PRAISE FOR *THROUGH STUDENTS' EYES*

"This project is groundbreaking and important: The authors used Youth Participatory Action Research, inviting youth to use photo-voice structures to share their perspectives and challenge traditional notions of youth identities. From a 'stance of humility and invitation,' Zenkov and Harmon's representations allow us to see their families, schools, and communities in new ways. This is a delightful and informative text that you will not easily forget." —**Deborah Appleman**, Professor of Educational Studies, Carleton College; co-author, *UnCommon Core* and Kathleen Hinchman, Professor of Reading and Language Arts, Syracuse University; co-editor, *Best practices in adolescent literacy*

"This book will provoke needed conversations among whole school faculties and their administrators about what school really means to young people in urban schools. For teachers of writing, it offers a pathway for students who may not seem to take to composition easily or automatically. There is something so powerfully practical about this approach, that I can already imagine teachers shouting '*Of course!* Let's do it!' The book also offers deeply compassionate and ethical insights into what truly matters to human beings." —**Randy Bomer**, Charles H. Spence Sr. Centennial Professor of Education; Director, Heart of Texas Writing Project, University of Texas-Austin; author, *Building Adolescent Literacy in Today's English Classroom*

"It is impossible to read the narratives and look at the accompanying photos of these youth on the margins and not feel the power of teaching through students' eyes. Zenkov and Harmon advocate a curriculum that invites youth to give form and voice to the big important issues in their lives that often go unaddressed in most language arts classrooms. With an equal balance of scholarship, sensitivity, and candor, these authors exhort teachers in this timely resource to create supportive contexts where students can name and deconstruct the barriers to academic achievement, and then envision possible selves and futures." —**William Brozo**, Professor, George Mason University; author, *Content and Disciplinary Literacy for Today's Adolescents* (in press)

"Zenkov and Harmon deliver a seriously considered call for rebalancing the perceived values of both the science *and* the art of creating a truly effective teaching and learning environment. They deliver a compelling invitation for all writing teachers, particularly those who work with struggling writers, to revisit the extent to which their practice incorporates an adequate focus upon the 'whole student.' [They] make a strong case for a unique paradigm shifting approach to engaging struggling writing students that begins with a respect for the myriad of 'beyond the classroom' variables that have influenced the students' perceptions of their abilities to describe the world as they have come to see it." —**Jerome Burg**, Founder, GLT Global ED; author, *BookMapping: Lit Trips and Beyond*

"The instructional approaches advocated in this book are deceptively simple: ask good questions, make images, talk and write about those questions and images. These practices, however, have the potential for radically re-centering young people's relationships with writing, schooling, and adults. It's not just *what* Jim and Kristien do but rather *how* they do it, revealed in story after story as a beautiful combination of humility and humanity. All kids should find what these authors call 'shelter' in the classrooms of such caring and reflective practitioners." —**Kelly Chandler-Olcott**, Laura J. & L. Douglas Meredith Professor for Teaching Excellence, Syracuse University

"*Through Students' Eyes* enacts as well as features a 'relationship-oriented approach' and a deep trust in youth to show us what we so often fail to discern about their experiences of school. Through the 'photovoice' structures Zenkov and Harmon provide, students who are typically disenfranchised capture their experiences and insights and, through their representations, both affirm themselves and educate readers. Vivid in students' words and images, this text invites educators to pay attention as youth show us how we need to learn to see anew." —**Alison Cook-Sather**, Director of the Teaching and Learning Institute, Bryn Mawr and Haverford Colleges; author, *Learning from the Student's Perspective: A Sourcebook for Effective Teaching*

"This amazing project offers both the educator and the student a wonderful opportunity. Teachers are able to view the authentic lives of their students and in turn connect more deeply. Students are given an opportunity to share a voice they may not even know that they have. Real writing. Real voices. Real gains. A must-read for every English teacher. . . . One of the most powerful writing projects I have encountered in my twenty-five years of teaching." —**Kelly Croy**, English Teacher (Oak Harbor, Ohio) and Apple Distinguished Educator; author, *Along Came a Leader: A Guide to Personal and Professional Leadership*

"*Through Students' Eyes* challenged me, as a reporter, to deepen the way I 'heard' youth in my community. I still borrow the techniques today. The methods honed by Zenkov and Harmon allow students to examine their identities and surroundings with unparalleled perspective. It opens the door for youth (and the caring adults in their lives) not only to discuss and consider the possible, but to understand the realities that support or hinder them in reaching their goals." —**Rachel Dissell**, reporter, *The Cleveland Plain Dealer*

"Action research at its most stellar and impactful. In this book, youth lead the way, drawing on multiple literacies to share their knowledge about what they know educators can and must do to recognize, revise, create, and nurture classrooms, schools, and systems of education worthy of their investment. Students' words and images speak forcefully here. Let's hope all of us are listening." —**Elizabeth Dutro**, PhD, Professor, Literacy Studies, School of Education, University of Colorado Boulder

"Redefining literacy in the secondary classroom, *Through Students' Eyes* crafts new entry points through visual (and/or media) literacy for all learners to tell their story. In this text we come to know a diverse group of young people faced with challenges and school experiences not typically heard, seen nor written about. Through pictures and photo story TSE captures the hearts and minds of teens while inviting them to tackle critical issues of identity, empathy and resilience. By engaging a multimodal, creative approach to writing, Zenkov and Harmon empower students to share their voice in a way that is authentic, relevant and significant. A moving invitation to voices not always heard, this book empowers urban youth to tell their story through image and purpose-driven writing. A must-read for urban educators, this book leverages media literacy to capture the hearts and minds of teens. In this inspiring read we see passion and purpose driven writing that empowers urban youth to tell their story. *This* is school!" —**Kristin Ziemke**, first grade teacher, Chicago; author of *Amplify: Digital Teaching and Learning in the K-6 Classroom*

Through Students' Eyes

Writing and Photography for Success in School

Also in the *It's Easy to W.R.I.T.E. Expressive Writing Series*

Through Students' Eyes

Writing and Photography for Success in School

KRISTIEN ZENKOV and JAMES HARMON

ROWMAN & LITTLEFIELD
Lanham • *Boulder* • *New York* • *London*

Published by Rowman & Littlefield
A wholly owned subsidiary of The Rowman & Littlefield Publishing Group, Inc.
4501 Forbes Boulevard, Suite 200, Lanham, Maryland 20706
www.rowman.com

Unit A, Whitacre Mews, 26-34 Stannary Street, London SE11 4AB

British Library Cataloguing in Publication Information Available

Library of Congress Cataloging-in-Publication Data
ISBN 978-1-4758-0809-4 (cloth : alk. paper) — ISBN 978-1-4758-0812-4 (paper : alk. paper) — ISBN 978-1-4758-0813-1 (electronic)

∞™ The paper used in this publication meets the minimum requirements of American National Standard for Information Sciences—Permanence of Paper for Printed Library Materials, ANSI/NISO Z39.48-1992.

Printed in the United States of America

Contents

About the *It's Easy to W.R.I.T.E.* Expressive Writing Series

Expressive writing originates in the writer's lived experience, whether past, present, or imagined future. Written in the author's own voice, expressive writing creates bridges between thought and feeling, reason and intuition, idea and action. It is equally rooted in language arts and social science, and it takes multiple forms: journals, poetry, life story, personal essay, creative nonfiction, song lyrics, notes, and snippets of thought. Expressive writing is democratic and accessible. No special knowledge is needed, supplies are available and affordable, and research confirms that outcomes can be profound and even life-changing.

The *It's Easy to W.R.I.T.E.* Expressive Writing Series captures the voices of worldwide experts on the power of writing for personal development, academic improvement, and lasting behavioral change. Authors are both theorists and practitioners of the work they document, bringing real-life examples of practical techniques and stories of actual outcomes.

Individually or as a compendium, the volumes in the *It's Easy to W.R.I.T.E.* Expressive Writing Series represent thoughtful, innovative, demonstrated approaches to the myriad ways life-based writing can shape both critical thinking and emotional intelligence. Books in the series are designed to have versatile appeal for classroom teachers and administrators, health and behavioral health professionals, graduate programs that prepare educators and counselors, facilitators of expressive writing, and individuals who themselves write expressively. Workbooks offer well-crafted, self-paced writing programs for individual users, with facilitation guides and curricula for anyone who wishes to organize peer writing circles to explore the material in community.

Each book or chapter author is held to exacting standards set by the series editor, Kathleen Adams. Prior to her 1985 launch as a pioneer and global expert in the expressive writing field, Adams served as chief editor for a non-fiction publishing company.

It's Easy to W. R. I. T. E.

What do you want to write about? Name it. Write it down. (If you don't know, try one of these: *What's going on? How do I feel? What's on my mind? What do I want? What's the most important thing to do? What's the best/worst thing right now?*)

Reconnect with your center. Close your eyes. Take three deep breaths. Focus. Relax your body and mind. Gather your thoughts, feelings, questions, ideas.

Investigate your thoughts and feelings. Start writing and keep writing. Follow the pen/keyboard. If you get stuck, close your eyes and recenter yourself. Reread what you've already written, and continue. Try not to edit as you go; that can come later, if at all.

Time yourself. Write for five to twenty minutes or whatever time you choose. Set the timer on your phone, stove, or computer. Plan another three to five minutes at the end for reflection.

Exit smart. Reread what you've written and reflect on it in a sentence or two: *As I read this, I notice . . .* or *I'm aware of . . .* or *I feel . . .* Note any action steps you might take or any prompts you might use for additional writes.

List of Figures

Chapter 1

Chapter 2

Chapter 3

Chapter 4

Chapter 5

Chapter 6

Chapter 7

Chapter 8

Chapter 9

Chapter 10

Foreword

KATHLEEN CUSHMAN

What makes school matter to youth? For sixteen years now, with the non-profit What Kids Can Do, I have asked that question of adolescent learners, transcribing their answers and combing their words to inform the work of teachers.

Some students speak of school as a holding pen where they wait to be released into their lives. Some split the screen: one side teeming with peer involvement; the other deadened by academic drudgery. Too few consider school a place where they reflect, communicate, act, and make new meaning—guided by adults who open doors to opportunity. Too many stay away until those doors close off to them.

When our subject turns to life outside of school, my informants also differ. Their circumstances sometimes offer shelter from the grievous pains of growing up. But often, these young people confront too much, too soon. They bear the burdens of adulthood without apprenticeship. No one invites them to interrogate their experience, to draw new purpose from it. The very adults in a position to do that—their writing teachers, for example—typically know little about their unseen lives.

Into this breach have stepped Kristien Zenkov and James Harmon to document their thrilling photovoice project, Through Students' Eyes. Across an impressive span of years, the curriculum they developed—part communication arts, part visual sociology—has proved substantive and actionable in a variety of educational contexts. In this book's remarkable and detailed account, Zenkov and Harmon show us just how their process deepens the thinking and widens the horizons of the adolescents they serve.

As the central task of this curriculum, young people take photographs in the worlds they occupy; especially, they look for shots that somehow bear on their attitudes toward school. An interested adult then sits with the photographer, jotting down the associations a chosen image carries for its taker. Those notes provide a scaffold for the student's writing, which centers on what the photo reveals about the place of school in that young person's life.

We can see several key strengths emerge in the youth who engage in this simple but revolutionary process.

First, they start to belong in a community of inquiry. Right from the start, individual photographs and introductions by name initiate each participant into an inclusive group with a common purpose. The subject of inquiry itself derives from community: *Who are we? Who might we become? What does school have to do with that?* Every request and activity signals interest, trust, candor, commitment, and respect for the student's competence.

Next, these youth begin to use their authentic voices. Achieving this outcome often seems to be a losing battle, in an academic world that prizes length and pedantry in writing. Yet to produce classic prose we must "talk first," as the humanities scholar Francis-Noël Thomas and the cognitive scientist Mark Turner (2011) remind us. If apprentice writers can *say* to an interested listener what they directly perceive—including their "inferences, judgments, predictions, cultural knowledge, in fact recognition of any sort"—then their writing can follow the same form, "clear and simple as the truth." That scenario sounds remarkably like the "elicitation conferences" that Zenkov and Harmon describe, where talking about their photographs offers young people an entry point to deepen their inquiry further.

When they finally put their insights into writing, even the most disaffected youth have just experienced a new relationship to school. In the examples that punctuate this book, they question, document, and analyze what forces might shape their identities as learners. Their written presentations—grounded in images, rendered with the immediacy of spoken language—ring "clear and simple as the truth."

Zenkov and Harmon culminate each photovoice project with an event at which students present their writing and photographs to an audience that includes teachers, relatives, friends, and younger students. The research and policy community, too, has much to learn from looking closely at this richly developmental approach to writing, on a subject of vital importance to us all. In the pages that follow, its transformative effects shine through the words and images of adolescents once unseen by our system of schooling.

—Kathleen Cushman, cofounder, What Kids Can Do

January 2016

Reference

Thomas, F.-N., and M. Turner. 2011. *Clear and simple as the truth: Writing classic prose.* Princeton: Princeton University Press.

Preface

Schools may be the most foundational of institutions in the United States, the primary thread through which our communities are woven together, and the only structure on which it seems everyone can agree our nation should invest and attend. Of course, "school" takes almost as many forms as there are neighborhoods across our vast nation. And our relationships to school and formal education vary widely and wildly from person to person, family to family, neighborhood to neighborhood, and state to state. But, it seems, *no one* really questions the existence of schools or their places in the fabric of our society.

Except that *some* people do—some of our most diverse and disenfranchised youths and community members *do* question the validity and nature of schools. But too many educators, other community members, and policymakers simply do not recognize or appreciate this skepticism or its complexity.

This is where this book and the Through Students' Eyes (TSE) project comes in: as teachers and teacher educators and community activists, we believe that these varied relationships to school must be acknowledged and that allowing youth to examine and share their perceptions of school may be the most effective manner of both better engaging our increasingly diverse student populations with school and of identifying necessary school structure, curricular, and pedagogical reforms that will make this institution a more relevant one.

A Personal, Professional, and Sociological Study

Through Students' Eyes was informed in a sociological sense by the schooling experiences with which we were most familiar—our own and those of our immediate family members. Our project and the pedagogies on which it relies were also guided by our own relationships with school. And, perhaps above all, the types of teachers we aspire to be—inside and outside of our TSE experiences—have been profoundly influenced by our own and Kristien's dad's experiences.

For Jim, these experiences translate into our pedagogies in very school-explicit ways. While he struggled in school much of the time, what did matter to him was clear: writing and photography. He was fortunate enough to be surrounded by books and a range of other texts and print materials during his upbringing, and the result was that he became a voracious young reader, even tearing through questionably appropriate Stephen King novels at the age of twelve.

As he entered high school, Jim became interested in first photographing, and later writing, for his school's newspaper. The newspaper's advisor, John Bowen, an English teacher, was very intentional about getting to know all of his student staffers. He trusted them to tackle real-world issues through their writing, and provided an experience that was foreign to Jim in comparison to what he had otherwise experienced—and disengaged from—in school.

You can imagine the improbable success story: Jim went on to become editor-in-chief and managing editor of the high school's newspaper, which profoundly contrasted with his performance in his classes. He won several awards for his writing and photography—further accentuating the dissimilarity between his demonstrated potential in school and a project that really *mattered* to him. Mr. Bowen has served as a mentor, friend, and model to Jim for almost three decades—even, naturally, as Jim became a high school teacher himself.

Kristien was aware as early as his elementary years that his dad was a highly intelligent, thoughtful, creative, and sadly frustrated individual—the latter condition almost solely the result of his school struggles. As the child of working-class parents with no history of college attendance, pursuing a postsecondary degree was an unlikely prospect for his dad from the start. But he attended college in fits and starts into his early twenties, and pulled back each time to support his own aging and ailing father—Kristien's grandfather.

Kristien's dad was painfully aware of the lifetime of missed opportunities he now faced as the result of this peripheral connection to school, and Kristien spent hours, days, and years engaging with his dad around all manner of artistic projects. Their close relationship allowed Kristien access to much of his dad's inner life, including the hopes for worldly success he still harbored, the extent of his intellect, and his natural role as a radical thinker. It is fair to say that eventually his dad's pain became Kristien's own, and he was determined that he would never face the same frustrations his dad had. In short, he would take advantage of every educational opportunity that came his way in order to make things right—for himself and, perhaps by extension, for his dad.

Thus was born Kristien's awareness of the importance of school and his own motivation to learn and succeed in school and, eventually, beyond it. But as a college student, Kristien soon recognized that he was as interested in his professor's pedagogies as he was in the content of any class. He understood that while his dad had never been able to focus much of his attention on his own schooling, he had grown very naturally into the most gifted of teachers. And Kristien was his primary student, in their hours of one-on-one interactions that so often revolved around authentic pursuits—art projects and his dad's inventions. And as Kristien transitioned from college to a consideration of a professional path, he recognized that his interest in providing educational opportunities—the ones on which his dad had missed out—might be satisfied by offering the same chances, the same extraordinary schooling, the same dynamic pedagogies to the most disenfranchised youth in America's schools.

Thus, through our lives as teachers and teacher educators, via our everyday interactions with youth and maybe most often via our implementation of Through Students' Eyes, we have longed to become teachers like Jim knew and Kristien's dad was—ones who use a relationship-oriented approach and trust youth enough that they might engage with school and our literacy tasks in ways beyond what these young adults and society in general have come to expect. The primary lesson we have learned since, via the Through Students' Eyes project, is that not only does our profession require a lifelong commitment to learning but also it is the students who are frequently the best teachers. Or at least the ones to whom we should be paying the most attention. And that making school a place where students want to be—by paying attention to their perspectives—is critical to reinforcing the importance of school itself.

What You Will Learn— A Preview of This Book

The Through Students' Eyes project grew not just from our personal and professional experiences with school and our awareness of our students' too often limited relationships to this institution and our curricula and pedagogies. In chapter 1, "Our Evolving Schools, Our Changing Students," we begin to detail the broader demographic shifts of US schools and communities. We offer discussions of the dropout, "pushout," and disengagement trends among our increasingly diverse youth, and we introduce the complicated ways in which adolescents' and their families' connections to school are related. We provide a summary of the TSE project and its photovoice structures, which illustrate how our schools and pedagogies must respond to the challenges today's teachers and students are facing.

Of course, it is not possible to offer a rich consideration of all of the contexts in which today's teachers and high school and middle school students are operating. But in chapter 2, "Picturing Cleveland, Seeing the United States," we look to the experience of Cleveland, a still shrinking and perpetually challenged Midwest urban center, as a lens on the difficulties virtually all of our US cities and many other communities are facing. Our experiences with diverse and disenfranchised youths are paralleling those of a growing number of teachers in the United States.

While one of the primary origins of our project were the disengagement realities we were witnessing in our students, we have discovered that our photo elicitation and visual sociology practices have roots in a variety of theoretical, teaching, and research traditions. We explore these in chapter 3, "The Foundations of Our Practices." These bases include notions of cultural relevance, the concept of multimodal literacy, research on student voice, and visually oriented and Youth Participatory Action Research (YPAR) methods. We also examine teaching practices and research that consider students' perspectives and voices as sources of information about schools, teaching, and curricula—methods that ultimately promote diverse youths' writing development.

In chapter 4, "Picturing a Writing Process," we detail the general implementation steps of TSE. We introduce some of the foundational writing instruction principles and methods we have developed through TSE, including the practice of Asking First, taking Class Pictures, developing a Class Quiz, and the Community Handshake activity. These strategies are rooted in notions of Blind Faith and Daily Forgiveness, which enhance teachers' abilities to help students recognize that the Apparently Mundane Matters.

Chapters 5 through 10 are all similar in structure, offering insights about our methods and about what our students have shared about a range of topics. In these chapters—as throughout the volume—we introduce and illustrate themes and strategies with youths' stories, images, and reflections. In chapter 5, "Picturing Self: Past, Present, and Future," we explore how the TSE project and its strategies allow students to know themselves as they are and to learn about the selves they want to be. We also share four additional foundational principles and practices of the project, linking our students' illustrations of "self" to the concept of Forgetting Our Writer Identities, the practice of Writing by *Not* Writing, and the Arc of Three Writing Conferences.

A key outcome of the project are sets of traits and habits these diverse youth would like to find in their teachers and structures they would like to see in their schools. In chapter 6, "Picturing Teachers and School," we highlight young adults' stories to detail pedagogical principles and teaching practices we have drawn from years of engaging with youth via our photo-driven writing processes. These include the idea that students' relationships with teachers are synonymous with their relationships to school; the fact that familiarity with students' cultures is not equivalent to having high academic and writing expectations of young people; the theory that writing teachers must engage *beyond* the classroom in order to build relationships in it; and the practice of coming in "sideways" with elicitation questions.

Our photovoice methods provide youths with important opportunities to identify—and begin to address—the challenges they are facing in their out-of-school lives. In chapter 7, "Picturing Challenges and Trauma," we wonder how these traumas, large or small, *cannot* impact students' relationships to writing and school. This chapter addresses a range of writing instruction principles and practices that honor these difficulties and help youth to work through them. These notions and strategies include the idea and practice of Explicitly Explaining the Assumed and Everyday, One-to-One or Not at All, Just Ten Minutes—Seriously, Ten Minutes, and Apparently the Mundane Matters.

Chapter 8, "Picturing Family and Community," includes a description of one of our former project participants, Neena, and her writing and photograph that detail how the relationship on which she counted most was with the man she called her stepdad. So many of our students demonstrated the unanticipated role that nonfamily "family" members, and the larger community, played in their lives and the impact they have on their writing relationships. This chapter also includes rich descriptions of our "photo walking" process, our practice of calling on students to write for and share with a community, and the notion that Writing Time Is Not Measured in Forty-Minute Periods.

Another of the most consistently appearing themes in our TSE participants' images and writings is the idea that teachers and schools must expand the notions of mentors and mentoring with which we are operating. In chapter 9, "Picturing Mentors and Mentoring," we detail how diverse young women and men in our project count on even those peers and adults in their lives who have failed to find school and worldly success as exemplars who can motivate them. We have discovered a number of mentor- and mentoring-related pedagogical and writing instruction insights, including the practice of Using Others' Images as a Way In and the idea that, as teachers, we must Fake It Until You Find It. Our most effective writing mentoring activities are rooted in the notion that in our classrooms there can be No Tourists, and that we might recognize what we now call the Mentoring Boomerang.

Finally, in chapter 10, "Picturing Success and Failure," we highlight some of the concepts of "success" and "failure" that TSE project participants have depicted and described in our work with them. These include the notion and orientation of a Stance of Humility and Invitation and the idea that we should never use Drive-By Assessments. They also include the practice of evaluating our students' writing through both Local and Global Assessments and the notion that our students' writing efforts are never done—they're just due.

Who Is This Book For?

It was in Cleveland, a decade ago, that we were awakened to these youths' potential and to the unique means of considering youths' points of view through images, as both a tool for engaging them and a vehicle for understanding better how to serve them. But the Through Students' Eyes project has become an increasingly relevant endeavor, not just for those of us in this challenged and challenging Midwestern city. It matters, too, for the veteran and future teachers with whom we collaborate and, we hope, for other city teachers and educators working with increasingly diverse and disengaged youth around the United States.

The crisis we are confronting may be especially stark in our city, but it is one that diverse and urban youth and their community members—and their teachers—around our nation are facing. Cleveland is a poster child for the state of our US cities and ex-urban centers, with its schools filled with a new and rapidly shifting population of diverse students. While Cleveland is where we began to *see* our students' perspectives and hoped to engage them at last in this thing we call school, we believe that if we could make sense of and begin to stem these trends in somewhere like Cleveland, then maybe we and others could do it anywhere.

This volume, then, is for any young people whose voices typically are not heard, whose images are not seen, whose stories are not told (by them), and whose writings are not read. We believe that this text is important, too, for youths who are *not* marginalized, but who would benefit from learning about other young people who have very different relationships to school than too many of us might assume. This text is also for any and all of the teachers of young people—those for whom school already works and for those for whom it does not—as it offers a compelling approach to school and writing instruction that will make this institution and some of its primary curricular emphases more relevant to virtually any audience.

Given who we are—teachers and teacher educators—we offer this text as a resource for future and veteran teachers, too. Primarily English and language arts teachers, but also for arts and social studies educators and others, too. We count our focus on youths' perspectives as a radical departure from the typical theories that ground our schools' curricula, and we hope that curricular theorists and other academics and thinkers will find our illustrations of these theories useful. Finally, as teachers, teacher educators, thinkers, and advocates, we intentionally intend to impact not just our own students, classrooms, and communities, but also larger trends and structures. We are confident that education and social policymakers would be informed by the methods and insights of this text.

This Place Called School

Our own "ways in" to school, the methods we offer to our TSE students, and tools of school, professional, and life empowerment that we believe we should supply to youth all begin with the multimodal approach to writing and writing instruction that we share in this volume. Echoing the perspectives of other educators and literacy theorists, we believe that *all* writing is personal and that every writing act is inseparable from each individual's writing identity, whether or not we are consciously considering such personas or connections while we are engaged in any element of a writing process (Gonzales et al. 2005; Zumbrunn and Krause 2012). We also believe that if we are to guide youth toward the deepest, healthiest, and most empowering of lifelong relationships to school and writing that we must provide them with opportunities to develop their own languages and voices, every day, in and out of our classes (Noguera 2008). We also believe that writing—or, more accurately, *composing*—is the most foundational of skills that we must facilitate our students in acquiring (Haddix and Sealey-Ruiz 2012). This latter conviction is not merely a case of subject-matter fandom, but an intentional, learned, and political conviction rooted in the reality that writing is simultaneously a *consumptive* and a *creative* act.

When we began our project, we had the wisdom to appreciate the potential application of a multimodal notion of literacy with youths who we thought likely would not be comfortable sharing their perspectives via traditional, language-focused inquiries (Connolly and Kress 2011; Gold 2004). After a decade of implementing our practice-based photovoice research project, we have contributed to a growing scholarly base that has documented how critical perspectives on youths' and families' and community

members' relationships to school and our literacy practices might be discovered through the use of alternative, visually oriented research methods
(Bell et al. 2011; Piper and Frankham 2007; Zenkov et al. 2013).

Our search for non-language-based methods ultimately led us to a consideration of photographs as text and a photovoice method, which has proven
effective for engaging diverse youths and for providing them with authentic
means to share their perspectives (Ajayi 2009; Bell 2008; Hicks 2013; Wang
2006; Zenkov and Harmon 2009). Image-based tools motivate students to
develop an awareness of and share personal insights related to their school
experiences (Doda and Knowles 2008; Smyth 2007; Zenkov et al. 2012). These
explorations have helped us and the audiences of our scholarship to understand factors related to the success and failure of students in our English language arts classes, while resulting in habits of thinking, reading, writing, and
speaking for youth that go beyond surface meanings and dominant myths to
understand sociological phenomena (Fobes and Kaufman 2008; Harper 2005;
Hibbing and Rankin-Erickson 2003; Zenkov 2009).

Ultimately, the TSE project is an existential endeavor: we are daring to
question the very existence of school and the teaching profession, while
simultaneously calling on the primary audiences of this institution—our students—to do the same. Our belief is that only by asking these questions will
we learn how to transform school into its most relevant form. And only by
providing typically disenfranchised students with tools to pose and answer
these questions themselves will they develop the academic efficacy and the
individual power and the civic capacities of which they are capable.

TSE is perhaps best understood as an approach that asks rather than answers a hopeful and metaphorically geographic set of questions. That is, we
inquire and we call on youth to inquire with us about what might be their
most effective and meaningful "ways in" to school. Making school a relevant
institution and helping youth to develop strong, positive connections to it is
akin to reading a map or making one's way through a maze. We believe that
every individual's "way in" to school is unique to them. And that the very
nature of the institution of formal education—the structures of schools, the
content of our curriculum, and forms of our pedagogies—should shift to enable students with these "ways in."

Our Evolving Schools, Our Changing Students

Evolving toward Indifference

FIGURE 1.1

"The Cartoon Network"

What makes me unsuccessful in school are video games and movies. Why? Because my favorite channel is the Cartoon Network, and I like to play video games. Sometimes when I like a show I get attached to the TV and hate when people interrupt me. Sometimes I forget to do my homework and hate that because I get bad grades. My parents never believed this year that I got good grades because I don't bring anything home from school. —Jose

Like what seemed the majority of our students, Jose appeared to be peripherally engaged in the middle school language arts class for English Language Learners (ELLs), where we met him several years ago. We were partnering with his teacher to implement our photovoice project, Through Students' Eyes (TSE), which called on young people to illustrate their perspectives on school with photographs and to write reflections on images that they felt best represented their points of view. He impressed us as being similar to so many of the young Latino men in our classes: he maintained a somewhat detached demeanor, and his academic performance was maddeningly inconsistent in spite of the positive rapport we had worked to build with him.

An outsider might have interpreted Jose's demeanor as evidence that he was an extraordinarily shy young man: he barely said anything in class. Yet—unwittingly or with whole-hearted intent—he completed just enough of his in-class tasks and not a single piece of homework, so that he was always perilously close to failing his language arts class. He seemed to instinctively know how to "do" school, both socially and academically, to the point that he gave the impression that he was choosing to live on the school edge, to lurk harmlessly in the shadows and the corners of his classrooms.

In our interactions with and observations of him at school, he always *appeared* to be on task. But when his teacher and we discussed his actual contributions after any given project session, we could never recall even one explicit statement he had made or a single particular assignment he had submitted. Without that closer examination, we likely would have described him as a quietly conscientious student—as one who generally applied himself to his school tasks.

It was only through the visually driven writing conferences and the unique products of the Through Students' Eyes photovoice project that we were able to look more closely at Jose and pay more attention to the specifics and truths of his place in school. It was via these elicitation conferences where he was able to provide written reflections similar to the one accompanying his image above that we came to appreciate that he often simply did not understand the assignments we gave him. By the very fact that he was an immigrant from

Central America, of Latino descent, and was still learning English, he was dramatically different than our own public school peers when we were middle and high school students in Midwestern US urban and rural settings.

It turned out that many of the quiet youth in the classes we now teach silently suffer through an almost perpetual confusion, feeling an unobtrusive but almost absolute academic desperation. Jose not only represented these voiceless adolescents but also complicated the picture we were encountering. He embodied the lightning-speed evolution of our community and the echoes of school disenfranchisement that we now recognize carries across generations of our community members. His statement about never bringing anything home from school spoke to the discouraging—even absurd—reality that too many teachers, everyday citizens, and policymakers simply do not appreciate: school is a very foreign place to an increasing percentage of our nation's youth and their families.

Not surprisingly, Jose preferred to communicate in Spanish inside and outside of our classroom, and he became respectfully but unambiguously agitated when he was forced to speak and write in English. To muddle his life and his questionable attachment to school further, Jose was often compared to his older brother, both at home and in our school building. His sibling also attended this middle school, and he was a very personable young man who seemed naturally inclined to find—or even create—trouble wherever he wandered.

Via another photograph and writing from our project, we later learned how Jose's brother's tendencies and reputation mortified him: Jose did not have a good relationship with any member of his family, and he resented the fact that his sincere (if limited) attempts to engage with school and the fact that he was avoiding the negative attention his brother actually seemed to enjoy went largely unappreciated at home. We invited Jose to participate in our project with the hope that he would discover some different and perhaps deeper motives for participating in school, learn to perceive himself as a capable writer and student, and maybe share and begin to understand some of the reasons why a formal education was a lower priority in his life and in his family's judgment than both he and we hoped.

The small community where we met and worked with Jose represented a different present and certain future of US schools. His mid-Atlantic ex-urban town had experienced considerable demographic shifts in the past decade, seeing a substantial increase in immigrant youth and moving from 5 percent to almost 35 percent ESOL students. These families were arriving from as close as a few miles away from the Washington, DC, inner-ring suburbs— where housing costs were ever-more unaffordable—and from as far away as Guatemala, El Salvador, Korea, Russia, Pakistan, and many other nations. While such rapid demographic changes might seem exceptional, they are, in fact, representative of the shifts in community makeup and schools' constituents that virtually every US teacher will face in the future (Cruz and Thornton 2013, Lucas and Grinberg 2008).

Through Students' Eyes: At a Glance

Founded in 2004, the Through Students' Eyes (TSE) project is oriented around the following contexts, ideas, practices, and products:

- Diverse, most often urban, and frequently English-language-learning youth comprise an increasingly larger percentage of our public schools' students; they are frequently disenfranchised and disengaged from school, evidenced by high school dropout or "pushout" rates that are consistently between 30 percent and 50 percent and often continue across generations.
- These diverse, disenfranchised students often do not appear to recognize the value of school and frequently struggle with literacy and writing tasks, but they are generally proficient with visual tools and texts—including photographs.
- The best sources for understanding these youths' perspectives on school and how teachers might support their school engagement and success might be young adults themselves.
- "Photovoice" methods and Youth Participatory Action Research (YPAR) techniques are engaging for diverse students, support their success with school and its traditional writing tasks, and provide key information about how to promote adolescents' attendance and achievement in school (Zeller-Berkman 2007).

- Implemented in English class and out-of-school meetings with more than seven hundred young people, Through Students' Eyes uses photovoice and YPAR techniques to explore diverse youths' perspectives on school, calling on them to address three questions with photographs and writings:

  1. What is the purpose of school?
  2. What things help you succeed in school?
  3. What things impede your school success?

- TSE participants typically engage in the project for ten project sessions, shooting ten to twenty-five images for each session via planned and open-ended "photo walks," eventually choosing three to five photos that they believe best answer the project questions, and writing and revising paragraph-length descriptions of the ideas represented by these pictures.
- The TSE project uses "photo writing" or "photo elicitation" conferences—supported by teachers, teacher educators, and preservice teachers—to help youth explore these images; these one-on-one conference structures allow youth to move past literal explanations and toward more metaphorical descriptions that are oriented around solutions to youths' disenfranchisement from school and enhance their writing development.
- The project has resulted in numerous authentic projects—exhibitions, publications, and presentations of images, writings, and analyses shared by youth participants and the project's teachers, directors, and mentors.

Dropping Out, "Pushing" Out

"What, Kay, What Do You Want?"

My father is a hardworking and respectful person. I can always talk to him about things that occur in school in general. He's always telling us about how he wishes he would have graduated from high school. My father inspires me to succeed in school because he encourages me to do well in school, so my life will be easier than his was and still is. My dad quit school a year and a half before he would have graduated because of his experience in the Cleveland school district. Before that he attended schools in Mount Pleasant, Pennsylvania and that showed him what it's like to be in a better and more organized school district, so it was very hard for him in Cleveland. When he finally made friends, busing took them away from him. Both of his parents were taken by the time he was 12, so when his friends were taken too he had no one to turn to for advice or dependency. That's why he dropped out. He had no common interests with the new group of people he was with and it was very hard to make new friends. My dad has struggled throughout his entire life. He has had to work multiple jobs for long hours to make ends meet. My dad is a strong person, but he is also tired and withered. I don't want the same thing to happen to me. My relationship with him has made things a lot easier for me. —Kayla

Kayla was an incredible spitfire of a young woman, someone about whom we had marveled often—a sixteen-year-old going on sixty who we sometimes thought was more capable of managing her life than we were our own. We met Kayla when she was a junior in the English class of Libbie Tompkins, one of the wonderful teachers who has welcomed us and the Through Students' Eyes project into his or her classrooms over the years. But it had been impossible in previous years, even before we started to work with her, *not* to notice Kayla around Rhodes High School.

While she likely had not grown in physical stature since she was in late elementary school (she stood all of about 4′8″), she opened a swath when she walked down the halls at Rhodes. Maybe it was the fact that virtually all of her peers towered over her and were momentarily stunned to find this little person moving toward them with such absolute confidence. Or maybe it was some of the not-so-subtle nuances of her appearance: she was a striking young woman, dressed most often head-to-toe in black with de rigueur silver studs protruding from various items of clothing and from various parts of her body, black nail polish and eyeliner, and generally pointy—even dangerous looking—pieces of "jewelry." She was not quite a lethal moving weapon like some "goth" youth, but she got your attention and made you unwittingly pause or flinch, out of what seemed a reasonable fear of being punctured or impaled.

Kayla also stood out because she was nearly joined at the hip to her friend Lindsay, another of the youth involved with the Through Students' Eyes project, and someone whose appearance generally mirrored Kayla's—

although Lindsay was physically closer to the average height of her peers. If judged by first impressions, most people, including teachers and their peers, might have deemed Kayla and Lindsay detached or even a bit hostile—certainly not approachable. Their "uniforms" alone suggested that these young ladies were dark, brooding, distant adolescents. But what was most evident about Kayla and Lindsay—particularly when they were together—was the fact that they were on a life-or-death, take-no-prisoners mission to succeed, inside every class and in every other context.

They were almost frightfully serious young women, and, like so many of our students, they were cautious with smiles. After not too many years as city teachers we learned that this might be one of the reasons why so many urban youth are judged so quickly and so harshly in their everyday encounters with the rest of society. When such young people are taught by individuals who did not grow up in the city—where smiling at anyone except the members of your inner circle is an unspoken sign of weakness—they can be appraised as disengaged students or even cold-hearted young people.

It's not that their teachers consciously think such things about these youth; we still speculate this "misreading" of young adults is the result of differences in experience, cultures, or class. Kayla and Lindsay were two young Caucasian women whose faces disclosed a maturity well beyond their years, earned from life events over which they had little control. They were young women who were not going to allow their peers, teachers, administrators, or even us to waste their time. They were going to let us know when they felt that anyone was daring to do this, every single time.

But as her image and reflection above reveal, it was Kayla's family, her parents' relationships to school, and her relationship with her siblings and her mom and dad that we remember most. After meeting Kayla's family, with her present, it seemed obvious that she was motivated by her inexplicable awareness of and frustration around the challenges it seemed everyone in her clan—except her—was facing on an almost minute-by-minute basis. We have never fully understood what in Kayla's life had driven her toward her tremendous school success; like so many of our students' families, hers was overwhelmed with merely surviving. She also was managing not only her own day-to-day existence but also attempting to do so for her parents.

It's almost as if every family is given a finite amount of worldly savvy, and Kayla had received every last morsel accorded her own. Perhaps even more accurately, Kayla had been born with, and had proceeded to develop, an awareness of this worldliness. She intended to use it for her own survival and achievement and for that of her family members, to whatever extent an underage, physically undersized but very determined teenager is able.

Kayla's family was profoundly—and yet typically—tested by the ravages of poverty. We only met her dad once, when he was with the family and picking Kayla up from the library after one of our photograph selection and writing sessions. He was cordial with a "hello," but stayed planted in his battered truck. At not-yet forty, he was almost completely disabled already and thus unable to provide for his family in the way that he longed to do and felt he should. He was supportive and loving of Kayla but physically pummeled. Kayla openly speculated with us that the state of her dad's body and psyche were the result of too many years of back-breaking days in minimum-wage jobs and some significant and undiagnosed disabilities that Kayla recognized were the result of her dad's birth to a mother on the verge of menopause.

Kayla's mom was more her friend than her parent, and Kayla knew she needed adult guidance. Her mom was kind to us, clumsily deferent, and just as absolutely supportive of Kayla as her dad. Mostly, though, she recognized that Kayla generally did not need her to interfere in her life: rather, she looked to Kayla for gossipy discussions and answers to the difficulties the family was facing. While this assessment of the state of her family might sound harsh, we are confident that Kayla would not disagree—she was not one to shy away from the truth, even when it so literally hit close to home.

Kayla's two younger sisters and brother were generally capable students and were finding some school success. But they were also struggling with mild learning disabilities and the low expectations often provided for them by their schools and the cycle of poverty and school disengagement into which they had been born. We did not know these siblings well—the oldest after Kayla was just starting high school when she finished—but Kayla cared about them deeply and talked about them as if they were her own children.

In retrospect it is clear that Kayla's complicated and loving relationships with her parents and siblings played significant roles in who she was and why she was pursuing school and life achievement the way she was, although anyone challenged to describe a linear relationship between Kayla's life experiences, her awareness, and her goals would be hard-pressed to do so. We knew her extremely well, and even we cannot begin to make a wholly accurate sense of these equations. And yet we know that this constellation of family members and issues was at the center of who she was and what she was pursuing.

Kayla's life—maybe best demonstrated by her dad's experiences—painfully illustrated the sad but too often ignored reality that, to so many diverse youth and their networks of friends and family, school simply does not mean what it does to many of their teachers and to the general public and our local, state, and federal politicians. Dropout—or "pushout"—rates are criminally high in so many of these cities, economically disadvantaged communities, and neighborhoods filled with increasing percentages of diverse, immigrant, and English-language-learning young people around our nation. Too often these youth simply disappear from school, not earning diplomas on anything akin to a traditional timeline, not five years later after returning for a General Equivalency Diploma (GED), not ever. Those who are "pushed" out are most often not *actively* done so. Rather, our archaic and unresponsive school policies and traditions, our curricula, our teaching practices, and our overwhelmed teachers simply cannot pay attention to another, even more hidden, population of adolescents. Particularly vulnerable are a population of young people who become less and less frequent attendees and increasingly infrequent participants in our classes, until they, too, disappear.

Often products of overlapping successions of teen pregnancy, these city students and their parents are characteristically less than half of a conventional generation's span apart (Alexander, Entwisle, and Kabbani 2001; Anyon 2006; Greene and Winters 2006). As a result, their adult family members' relationships to school and its literacy practices are almost synonymous with these youths' own rejections. We fear these adolescents will eventually share these denials with their own children (Erickson et al. 2007).

The outcome is that parents', adult family's and community members', adolescents', and the next generation's relationships to school and their rejections of formal education are intricately interwoven and difficult to interrupt (Bridgeland, Dilulio, and Morison 2006; Ladson-Billings 2007; Orfield et al. 2004). Many reports on high school dropouts—or, again, "pushouts," which often seems a more accurate term, given their frustrating school experiences—have exposed how the cross-generational nature of school detachment has advanced an exponential boost in the pervasiveness of an "unschooling" stance among so many young people (Samuelson 2004).

When we initially asked Kayla about what she thought of school, her reactions echoed those of most of our students and, we venture, those of most urban, disenfranchised, often English-language-learning and economically disadvantaged youth around the United States. Kayla actively complained about what she perceived as the irrelevance of the texts teachers use, the assignments we require, and the very nature of the institution where we daily met her and her peers. In some settings, these students' laments might be merely bothersome or could be dismissed as this generation's academic rite of passage. But for Kayla and too many of our most diverse students, these laments are merely the aftershocks of an earthquake of school detachment (Balfantz and Legters 2004, Orfield 2004). These criticisms and the dropout statistics in too many of our schools reveal a void in the traditional high school curriculum and an apparently deterministic—though reasonable—perspective that many youth have on school (Bridgeland, Dilulio, and Morison 2006).

Knowing and Honoring Our Students' Stories

FIGURE 1.2

"Love-Hate Relationship"

This picture answers the question: "What gets in the way of our success in school?" That answer is: addiction. Have you ever felt addiction? Have you ever felt that constant need, that constant want for the thing you can't get? Cigarettes, marijuana, alcohol; they trick you, and keep you coming back for more. This picture is of my cigarette that I stuck into the table. I kept it there, and watched it burn away. I wanted to save it, but at the same time I wanted it to die. It's a love/hate relationship. It's an abusive relationship. I challenged myself, and it hurt to watch it disappear, but I felt stronger when it was gone, as if one of the shackles of addiction had broken off one of my wrists. Sometimes I can't focus at school. I can't finish my homework without thinking about how calming it would be to have just one cigarette, but I refused. I want to succeed. I want to go on in life happy, and calm. Cigarettes don't make me happy. They don't make me calm. Anger builds up in my mind every time I light up, and the word "failure" flashes across my path, but I can't put it down. My mouth is metal and the cigarette is the magnet. "This can't go on," I tell myself, "but it will be so painful. It'll hurt too much. It can't be that hard. I can stop now. I can stop next week. I can stop next month." The time goes on and I begin to wonder, will I ever stop? In this picture, the cigarette towers over me. It's bigger than me, and I cannot defeat it. I cannot knock it down; I cannot break this. It controls everything about me, and it's killing me. Stopping for a while is out of the question, but quitting is not. Every day I will get stronger, and everyday this cigarette will get smaller. Every time I pick up a cigarette I think about school and my dreams, and my future. I am a strong addict, but this addiction is stronger. —Breanna

Breanna was a sophomore when we met her in Jim's English class at Euclid High School, in a small, struggling city that borders Cleveland to the east. She was painfully introverted and mouselike quiet, to an extent we have rarely encountered in our combined forty-plus years as city teachers. She barely uttered a word in class, let alone in our private conversations about school and her writing, except on the rare occasion when she decided that our composition topics were worthy of her consideration. Breanna was typically dressed in a manner that matched her blend-into-the-background mentality, an approach that was mirrored by her general reluctance to participate in class conversations and activities.

But it turns out that this shroud of "studenting" absolutely contrasted with who Breanna was beyond the school walls. She was essentially another parent to her toddler brother, and she spent more hours than we were able to tabulate supporting her mother in providing child care after the school day was over. Perhaps not surprisingly, we were not the only ones who had failed to know the real Breanna: her peers responded with jaw drops and appreciative expressions of "Damn!" when Jim first read her writing out loud to the class. None of us had any reason to expect to hear the poetic undertones of Breanna's writing or to appreciate the "other" tortured identity she was living.

The epitome of an old soul, it seemed Breanna stunned everyone—us, her peers, maybe even herself—when she showed an almost religious devotion to work on our then still-new Through Students' Eyes photography and literacy project during one of its early iterations. While she attended *every* meeting day, she maintained a reserved—or perhaps skeptical or sometimes even hostile—composure in virtually every interaction with us. As very veteran teachers, we knew enough to appreciate that adolescents who have found little else but frustration in school would likely still struggle to engage in an open-hearted manner even with teachers who exhibited genuine care or with projects that sincerely mattered to them. Sadly, that is one of the conundrums of too many city youth: they respond even to positive learning experiences like children depicted in case studies of the abused, who long for positive attention but never quite trust such kindness when it appears. Still, she clearly recognized something of an opportunity in TSE and its combination of photography and reflective writing, and she revealed her devotion to the project by taking and writing about images regularly.

Breanna's pictures and the ideas she shared through these visuals were among the most carefully considered we have encountered from the more than eight hundred youth with whom we have conducted TSE over the past eleven years, but never once did they seem staged or clichéd. When, in her intelligently guarded way, she began to trust us, she was hungry to share the realities that she was encountering in her life beyond our teacher purview. She offered the photograph and drafted the writing above with an intentionality and laserlike clarity of purpose. And she slipped in this combination as if she were testing us, even baiting us, to see if we were paying attention, to gauge how we would respond.

More importantly—to us then and to the project that is the focus of this book—Breanna shot many pictures and reflected deeply and with a level of awareness that we had not previously observed in her. It turned out that she was fully cognizant of what she thought her teachers needed to know and how school, including our English classes, might be reorganized in order to serve her better. She longed for school structures and schedules that would support (or at least allow) her family's child care and other daily life needs and thus enable her and our other students to focus more on our English class activities and school in general.

For us—teachers and teacher educators working in increasingly diverse high schools and economically impoverished communities—stories like Breanna's are all too common. And at the same time, lives and narratives like hers are all too infrequently considered when we think about the various issues of schooling—standardized tests, standardized curricula, standardized and scripted lessons, even standardized standards. Of course, Breanna was something of a poster child for our students today. But the reality is that too few of the adults and institutions that are supposed to be supporting them appreciate—really *know*—that these young women and men are faced with economic, family, and health concerns that keep them and their peers from focusing on school.

This is the lesson Breanna taught us, which is so relevant to teachers of diverse youth across the United States: our students are living lives that do not mirror our own, and we must consider their realities, very intentionally and very often via our pedagogies, if we are going to be able to help them find success in school and beyond. We know now that school and its foundational language simply do not mean to these youth and their families what they do to many of us, their teachers, the majority of whom are White, native English speakers (Sleeter 2008). We must explicitly invite students' lives into our English/language arts class activities.

The Pain of Lost Potential

"There Are Possibilities"

This young man is an artist in the community. He is living proof that not everything is bad in our society. He is an inspiration, not only to me, but to the younger kids. He shows us that there are possibilities out there. —Samantha

FIGURE 1.3

Samantha ("Sam") was one of most prolific photographers in our project. When we were still running film through 35 mm cameras, she shot more than forty rolls. She was one of the few students who really took our advice about taking her camera everywhere. She had access to situations that we most often could not imagine, and, to her credit, photographed *all* of them.

One of the images that Sam did not have to take—one of the phenomena that we did not need depicted via any other means—was of her school and specifically her classroom context. We began to work with her English class during her sophomore year, when students in this honors section numbered approximately twenty-five. By the time this group had reached what would have been their senior year, the class enrollment had shrunk to approximately fifteen, with a few of those who were still attending school doing so only on an erratic basis.

This often sudden and otherwise steady shrinking of entire high school classes is still something that rattles us. While we did not grow up in communities or attend high schools where academic achievement was particularly valued, graduating from high school was still the norm. We were always surprised by those three or four—out of a few hundred—students who dropped out at various points during our junior and senior years.

Even though we have taught and lived in these intense urban communities for decades, we were still almost dumbfounded when we saw that even students classified as "honors" level in a city high school found it absolutely ordinary to drop out of high school as soon as they knew the truancy police would not hunt them down for doing so. It was evident—and baffling—to us that these young people simply had not discovered or been offered a reasonable rationale for remaining in school. As foundational an institution as school might be to the vast majority of us in the United States, it was irrelevant to so many of our students.

Sam both represented and depicted the dramatic demographic shifts in places like this community, which closely mirror those in other urban areas as well as in many rural and ex-urban contexts around the United States. Whether these increasingly diverse youth are part of families who have lived in these communities for generations, are moving from more to less expensive neighborhoods and from suburb to suburb, or have recently immigrated to the United States, they are united by at least one factor: they were born into clans, communities, and networks that through no fault of their own do not have the foundations of positive relationships to school to help orient them toward academic engagement and achievement. Too many of our increasingly diverse youth simply are not sure about the purposes of this thing called "school."

Concentrating on our students' dropout and achievement statistics did little to inform us of the causes behind or the solutions to this embedded community relationship to school (Cook-Sather 2009; Erickson et al. 2007; Fine and Weis 1998). But engaging with these youth around images and subjects that they chose gave us tremendous insights into both the sources of and effective responses to these negative trends. Numerous educators, theorists, and researchers have explored the complexity of diverse urban youths' relationships to school (Anyon 1997, 2005; Barton 2005; Lareau 2003), revealing that these relationships never exist in a vacuum. And understanding these relationships—from youths' perspectives—must be our starting point.

We have learned to pay attention to the foundational question of the role of school in these students' lives and the ways that they learn to reject these formal educational institutions (Doda and Knowles 2008, Easton and Condon 2009, McClung 2002, Smith and Fasoli 2007). We now turn the question of the validity of the schooling venture back on itself and look to the intended constituents of schools for insights into this equation. Not only might they offer some of the most valid and relevant answers to the question of the purposes of school, but also their very act of responding might promote their engagement in these formal educational activities.

But we do not just call on youth to consider school's purposes and value via traditional research methods or just with words. Rather, we invite them to respond to these inquiries with pictures, so that we all might see and be able to respond to what our students believe. Even better, by looking to the images that represent their answers—visual evidence of their relationships to school and the impediments to and supports for their success in these schools—we might begin to *see* the ways in which we can make schools the sites of relevance and hope that we all desire.

We are thrilled and proud that Sam has recently completed a master's degree in education at a Cleveland-area college and is working in her first teaching position. She is still focused on the potential in herself and her community. Of course, potential may be an almost impossible quality to measure, but when the gap between one's promise—as a student, a citizen, a parent or partner, or in a career—and what one actually achieves is almost absurdly huge, it's a difficult thing to accept. Sam's image and writing above suggest that she was painfully aware of the potential in *all* of her peers, even those who many audience and community members would view as looking for trouble rather than holding academic and worldly promise.

Ultimately, the Through Students' Eyes project, this book, and our very teaching lives are driven by a desire to understand how such gaps occur and how we might span them. We are also driven to mitigate (and, we hope, eventually end) the tragedy that is a young adult who has untapped capacity but through no fault of her own simply does not yet know how to match her abilities with actual success. While we attempt to honor students' stories via this project and its unique writing instruction practices, we may never have an innate understanding or develop a lived knowledge of our students' perspectives or experiences. Yet we intentionally, stubbornly continue to recognize that so many of them are painfully aware that something else exists for them: something positive, something that a formal education and our project and these image-driven writing activities might allow them to access and share.

Picturing Cleveland, Seeing the United States

Schooling in the Margins

FIGURE 2.1

"Another Great Teacher"

When I look at this picture I see two different lives: I see a happy security guard, Michelle, and I see Mrs. Miller, a teacher who looks unhappy to be there.

19

For people who know Mrs. Miller, this is not the teacher we've seen over the years at Lincoln-West. She's usually happy all the time. . . . Students who have graduated still come back to get advice from her. I don't know if she's unhappy because of the recent layoffs or the sudden change in the school with the new staff. It would be a shame to see a good teacher like Mrs. Miller all of a sudden quit. I feel this can affect students because that'll be another great teacher we would have lost along with her support, honesty and friendship. —Maurice

Maurice—or Reese, as he was known—described his teacher, Mrs. Miller, and a school security guard, Michelle, as key supports for his success in school. We met all three of these individuals at Cleveland's Lincoln-West High School, where we first began the Through Students' Eyes (or TSE) project. At the time that Reese took this picture, any reasonable assessment of his transcripts would have suggested that he was *this close* to finishing high school. But that is one of the dangerous truths we learned through our work in Cleveland and that we now know to be valid for so many of our diverse and urban youth: we have to be careful never to assume too much about their appreciation for school, their understandings of its workings, or even their evaluations of their achievements—even when they are merely days away from graduating.

Sadly, in the ten-plus years since we began TSE, we have lost track of more of our Cleveland students than we can count. Contrary to what many observers who have not spent much time in city schools might expect, far too many of these young people had showed clear and consistent abilities to master any academic challenge we posed to them. And tragically, too many of these same very academically capable youths were like Reese, who was shocked to learn, in the very month he expected to graduate, that he was still short of credits. Eventually he had to claw through summer school after his senior year to earn his diploma.

Since our interactions years ago with Reese around his struggles to finish high school, he has drifted in and out of our lives with a frustrating regularity. Just when we thought we could stay connected enough with him to help him finally pursue a satisfying college or career path, he would make a choice that resulted in another temporary vanishing act. We have worked diligently, lovingly, to keep in touch with him, and we have attempted multiple times to help him enroll in a local community college. We have assisted him with the tangled web of financial aid applications and agreed to serve as a reference for a string of limited-wage jobs for which he has applied.

We appreciated the room Reese gave us to know him while we were his teachers, and he confirmed over and over again that he was a bright, sometimes painfully but silently sensitive young man. He had intelligence in spades, regularly shared with his friends a sense of humor delivered with a subtlety that made it almost impossible to reprimand him in class for doing so, and was one of the most creative filmmakers in Jim's video production class. He was a "good" kid who was derailed over and over by what might have been characterized as a classic "underachiever" profile. Cleveland, it seemed, had more than its fair share of such frustrated, intelligent youth—but we know many other teachers, families, and communities around the United States who face the same achievement enigmas.

But Reese possessed little confidence in his own intellectual or "school" abilities and did not seem to know how even to begin to consider his future, even as the end of his mandatory school "sentence" was approaching. We eventually came to understand this challenge as similar to that faced by adult second-language learners. They look as if they should be more than capable of accomplishing something seemingly so basic as having conversations in a community's predominant tongue. So, of course, they feel diminished senses of efficacy when they face and fail at these "shoulds." But it is simply not reasonable for anyone, young or old, to appreciate the story of why school matters if they are not even familiar with the language of its operation.

Jim revealed to Reese a few years later—when we had been repeatedly thwarted in our attempts to help him—that Reese reminded Jim of himself. That disclosure simultaneously made the soft spots in our hearts for Reese that much more tender *and* frightened us silly: Jim had graduated from high school a few decades prior with a 1.6 grade point average. While we both engaged with Reese in and out of school during his senior year, Jim has gone the extra mile in the decade since, long after Reese had begun to fade from our lives. Still identifying as Reese's teacher—and a profoundly committed one at that—Jim has spoken with Reese's mom on numerous occasions in the span of the past ten years, most often when she seemed to be able to do little more than echo our frustration.

"I don't know what to do with him anymore, Mr. Harmon," she would say. "My brother in Chicago is willing to help pay for Reese to go to school. But he doesn't seem to care."

Once, on his birthday, Reese disappeared for several days, not just from us but also from his entire network of friends and family. His mother called Jim in a panic, asking if he'd talked to him recently.

"He's been hanging around the wrong crowd, Mr. Harmon. I don't know how to handle it. I'm worried about him," she admitted.

We confessed that we were equally stumped. We were increasingly conscious of the fact that Reese was now in his early twenties, someone who we believed should be making his own, constructive, decisions. Yet he was like so many of our students, young people who simply seemed never to have learned how to do so. We talked through the fact that as much as we hoped for Reese's future, it was not reasonable or useful to blame him for his repeated life missteps. We acknowledged how we had naively anticipated years prior that his involvement with TSE would augment—or shake—his foundations enough to make a difference in the life path that we were now, almost helplessly, watching him travel.

Of course, our story of Reese does not end there. We continue to reach out to him when we can, and he is religious about contacting Jim, most often via text message, on Jim's birthday and on Father's Day. More importantly, so many of our Cleveland students mirror this brief arc of Reese's life. It is not a tale with an unequivocally happy ending, at least not yet. We must be clear: we are *not* suggesting that a deterministic perspective is the only one teachers working with diverse, disenfranchised youth can have on their students—in Cleveland, which we consider the poster child of communities filled with these young adults, or anywhere.

Reese and his story represent some of the most troubling realities of Cleveland, so many US cities, and other increasingly diverse and ever more economically impoverished communities. And this account of Reese speaks to our very personal motivations behind the work of the TSE project. We know now that often we cannot see these realities but through the lens of an individual, via the close chronicling of one young person's experience. And we believe that through an account of one urban context—one of our nation's most challenged communities, the city of Cleveland—the broader audiences of our schools' constituents might be able to grasp and solve these crises.

This is one of the truths of diverse adolescents' relationships to school that Reese and our Cleveland experience illustrates almost too well: youth and their families live on the fringe not only of our economic system but also of our education system. Very smart, very talented, and otherwise very capable young people and their networks of siblings, cousins, parents, and significant others are bewildered by schools' operations to the point that they are unaware even that they are on the outside looking in, until it simply seems far too late to learn school's language, norms, and rules. They respond with a very reasonable, unwitting self-preservation impulse, determining that school is just one more institution that is just not for them.

Seemingly Simple, Absolutely Complex Relationships to School

FIGURE 2.2

"The Alley Behind My House"

This little girl lives two doors down from my house. Drug dealers live in the neighborhood, and the alley is where they sell drugs. One time my brother was riding his bike there, and he saw prostitution going on. People running from the police always go through there. It's dangerous for her to be playing there. When I was that age, there used to be volunteers who would play games with us in the park. That program helped keep us out of trouble. It's not there anymore. —Sam

Samuel, or Sam, was of Argentinian descent, which was a considerable rarity among our students in the Cleveland communities where we were working and living. Lincoln-West had a huge Latino/Latina population. These youth were, in fact, the largest demographic in the school—the majority "minority." But nearly all of these young adults were at most one generation removed from life in Puerto Rico, with a smaller percentage of adolescents from Mexico and other Central American nations. Sam was a particular conundrum: he stood out from the crowd almost by blending into and through the masses.

We speculated that maybe it was the fact that he was not from one of the more common nations of origin of our students that made him seem so foreign much of the time and why his perspective on our community mattered so much. Of course, there was logic to such a perception. He looked the part of the average student in our United Nations of high schools, but he held secrets that suggested that he was just visiting, just hiding innocuously among us, just biding—though not wasting—his time among his peers and teachers. It was through Sam and our teaching lives in Cleveland that we became so painfully aware of the grand gap between what appeared to be true about our students and what actually were the realities of their lives and points of view.

Sam's parents had moved from Argentina when he was just a young boy, and the family visited their native land often. It was clear that his US clan was still very tied to their home country, and that theirs was a particularly tight-knit circle. They were a unit that was inexplicably, almost completely, immune to some of the negative norms by which they were surrounded. Sam was incredibly yet almost surreptitiously close to his sister. She was undoubtedly a mentor to Sam, and she was already a college graduate, so she was serving as the model for success for which he, like virtually all of our students, was so hungry.

Maybe that is why Sam was so poised for success: he, like his peers, was starving for roads to achievement, but with his sister close by his appetite was at least vicariously sated. She and Sam's family provided him with an obvious and apparently unshakeable foundation of which he seemed to be wordlessly but explicitly conscious. Perhaps most noticeably, he carried himself like a man on a mission, and he appeared largely impervious to the everyday social pressures felt so pointedly by his peers.

While Sam had plenty of friends at Lincoln-West, he just never seemed to fit in: he was quieter than your average high school junior or senior (Jim called him "Silent Sam"). He was also much more contemplative and willing to consider the bigger questions we were posing for him, and he just appeared to assume that he should be taking school very seriously. He did not openly declare to us or his friends just how different his perspective on school was, but it was obvious that he was an alien of sorts.

To us, Sam's image of this little girl in the alley remains one of the saddest and most compelling of any taken by students in the Through Students' Eyes project over the past ten years. Sam's place as something of an observer—an astute, seemingly distant spectator but actually a deeply engaged witness—was affirmed by another photograph he took and upon which he reflected, of a local playground that had been vandalized. The everyday realities of a city in deep distress that he depicted poignantly represented contexts that seemed incapable of supporting school structures and traditions that would enable any but the most exceptional young person to succeed.

"Reforms" and Rejections

"A Sense of Reality"

Today is moving mighty fast and I tend to lose a sense of reality. When I feel like giving up I think towards the future. If I don't stay in school and achieve the goals I've set for myself, where would I end up a couple of years from now, working a low-paying job maybe having two jobs trying to keep my family happy. Money doesn't give me happiness but it sure helps. No money means stress living a life I prepared not to live. I look at my mother and father; they barely have any education and they work hard and sometimes things get taken away. You could see in their eyes their unhappiness. I refuse to live a lower class life. . . . With the money problems [I see], I just feel like working all day long—quitting school and just getting a job. I'm only 17 and I'm still in high school. I shouldn't be worried about money problems. Last year I worked almost eight

hours a day, five days a week. I would come home at 11:00 pm and do homework until about 12:30 am. When the sun rose and my alarm rang I would be
so tired I would fall back to sleep. 30 minutes before I had to leave I would get
up. In class listening to my teachers "blah blah," my eyes got heavier, and I was
fighting them. Sometimes I ended up falling asleep. —Cynthia

Cynthia was involved with the third iteration of our project, in another Cleveland high school—James Ford Rhodes—that for years had been recognized as
the jewel in the district's crown. The school had quite a proud history, with its
graduates including comedian Drew Carey and its now sealed-off basement
track once a training site for Olympian Jesse Owens. Cynthia represented the
new neighborhood: she was a young woman of Puerto Rican descent, born in
the United States, and quite at home in Rhodes's diverse culture. Like many of
her classmates who participated in TSE that year, she was a school "survivor":
her original freshman class had shriveled to approximately half its size by the
time she and her peers were in their late junior and early senior years.

Kristien spent many after-school photovoice sessions with Cynthia, considering her images and ideas. She was a beautiful young lady and a bright,
occasionally sharp-tongued Latina. She did not appear to have a deep appreciation for the reflective work we were asking her to do through the TSE
project. But she engaged dutifully, more often than not offering diarylike
insights into her world and challenges. Of course, these personal minutia of
her existence proved to be very telling, and Cynthia's simple recounting of her
family's and her own financial struggles reminded us of how all-consuming
these realities can be. Her blurry image of a wad of cash on a coffee table that
accompanied her reflection above also reminded us how a seventeen-year-old
should not be so concerned with paying her own or her family's bills—certainly not to the point that she is actively, daily, contemplating dropping out
of high school.

As with the other young people whose stories we share in this chapter,
Cynthia and her family were, in many ways, representative of the troubles
faced by our larger community. They were part of the growing number of
economic and educational "have-nots" among our most diverse, English-
language-learning, and immigrant neighbors. Cleveland had been especially
hard hit by the economic crises of the end of the first decade of the new mil-
lennium. In 2000, the city was (and largely remains today) an urban center

dealing unsatisfactorily with its own history. Perhaps more so than any other major metropolitan context in the United States, it is one whose failings are inescapable, even tangible.

At the time we started TSE, downtown Cleveland was, and in many ways still is, a veritable ghost town, in spite of significant but sporadic efforts at revitalization. The focus of these efforts always appears to target the city's immediate core. Brand new condominium developments pop up in the middle of a sea of vacant parcels of land so numerous that their only value is as occasionally used surface parking lots. Stunning architectural examples built by the likes of Rockefeller swim amid an entire neighborhood of homeless shelters. The Cuyahoga River—which, it seems, no one outside of the city can forget has caught on fire not once but nearly a dozen times—flows slowly between the downtown and the west side, reminding everyone that this shrinking metropolis is starkly divided by race and region.

Not surprisingly, the city's schools are perpetually under reform, confronting a contracting student population and a continually diminishing tax base while attempting to serve an increasingly diverse demographic. The community continues to face that proverbial knife, violently cutting both ways—with the simultaneous shrinking of the city's student body and the fact that a substantial percentage of the high school population still disregards school as a viable learning, life, or professional option. The schools have perhaps been most challenged in recent years by three factors, which represent both long-term and immediate crises in our community and echo phenomena in other contexts around the United States.

The first is the history of segregation and busing that came to a head in the late 1960s, when federally mandated internal redistricting attempted to merge the isolated populations of wealthier White and poorer Black children and youth. The longest-lasting result of this effort was not integration and a rising tide of academic performance and economic achievement but perhaps the most complete example of "White flight" to a city's suburbs in our nation's history. Cleveland has become one of those places where everyone is *from* but fewer and fewer people actually *live*. While recent gains have been made in attracting a younger, more professional crowd to downtown Cleveland apartment and condominium vacancies, city neighborhoods continued to deteriorate. And the Cleveland Metropolitan School District keeps on withering as even Black families flee to the suburbs or charter schools.

The school district also continues to face two other examples of well-intentioned but apparently misguided government interventions. Some twenty years after mandated busing began, the city made another attempt to stem the flow of its wealthier constituents to surrounding communities and to address an era-long record of low student performance. The mayor disbanded the elected school board in the 1990s, was given the power to hire and fire its "Chief Executive Officer," and allowed the city government to appoint a community board. In a devoutly Democratic city that prides itself on neighborhood identity, this stifling of community members' voices has resulted in an even greater level of disengagement from the schools. The consequence is one that can be seen across the United States: it's just not clear who "owns" Cleveland's schools anymore.

Finally, that notion of "ownership" has another, more complicated, and often sinister meaning. At about the same time that the mayor took control of the schools, Cleveland began one of the country's first experiments with charter and voucher school funding mechanisms. Its traditional public schools continue to attempt to survive amid a flood of largely unregulated for-profit but still publicly funded educational organizations that appeal to the most desperate of parents who long for centers of positivity, safety, and academic success for their children. Instead, local and corporate educationist shysters who operate bare bones, computer-based instructional academies that line their own and their shareholders' pockets mostly serve these families. As predicted by virtually every critic, those vouchers—which represent the basic financial investment the city and state make in a child's education—are grossly insufficient as tuition subsidies for enabling economically deprived youth to attend better-performing private and religious schools.

These "reforms" are ones that many of our largest, most often urban, and most diverse school districts have implemented in the past few decades. And too often these "restructuring" efforts—which on the surface appear to be attempts at improving how schools might serve our most challenged communities—actually feed a cyclical, almost inescapable perception that schooling simply does not matter. The result in Cleveland—and too many other communities with similar demographics—is that the entire venture of schooling seems like a foreign invader—like some sort of ominous indoctrination that the locals deem an incursion on their rights rather than an institution that serves their children's and their community's short- and long-term well-being.

Even the "Buildings" Are Failing Us

FIGURE 2.3

"Having Fun"

Teens like to have fun with other teens and it is healthy to get out to enjoy yourself for just those couple hours. It helps you relieve stress. First thing Monday morning I wake up at five o'clock and get my little sister up and ready for school, get her down to the rapid station by six and then I come back home and make sure that my younger brother and another younger sister get up and dress by six forty-five. My younger brother and I leave to catch our bus and we get to school about seven thirty or seven forty. I call both of my sisters' schools and make sure that they made it there safely before I go to my first class. During athletic seasons I go to practice after school then head to work at five thirty then I head home at ten and get there about eleven. Before going to bed at eleven forty-five or midnight, I help my mom with her daycare and help clean around the house. —Markus

Markus was a kid who you prayed would succeed, because he was just that nice of a young man. He was someone who would look you in the eye and seemed to assume the best, day after day, even about the least committed of his teachers. He was always smiling, always cracking a joke, always throwing out a borderline-school-appropriate insult to his male peers. As his reflection above reveals, he clearly led a difficult life—one that required him to manage a schedule at which many adults would balk.

Yet in spite of this nearly impossible daily agenda, Markus was almost always in school and was quick to greet us with a handshake or the more involved and choreographed grip known as "dap." Our sense was that he, like so many of our students, was an old soul. He knew his life was complicated, he knew he should not be responsible for so many other people and so many tasks, and yet he never complained about these realities. Perhaps it was his natural optimism that led him to actually embrace the intensification with which he was dealing, and to pile on by joining our TSE project.

Markus's images tended to focus on what he considered the engaging aspects of his educational life—school dances, athletic events, friends at the lunch table, and more. But he provided many clues to us and his other teachers about what we should be thinking about as we were attempting to plan the most relevant and effective lessons. It was evident that Markus was in a groove, and the still new adult responsibilities that he shared with his mother made a peculiar sense and held a particular appeal to him. Yet like most city students, he was a heartbeat away from his world collapsing from any number of factors, big and small—all of which were outside of his adolescent control.

In what might seem like the most obvious of comparisons, Markus's tenuous life balance and clear promise were beautifully, painfully representative of the untapped capacity of Cleveland and so many cities and other communities like it. In spite of its history and the seemingly endless number of factors impeding its progress, Cleveland remained a place that almost no one visited without noting that it seemed to have untold potential. It boasted a lakefront location, no worse weather than a thriving central US metropolis like Chicago, and a hybrid of East Coast and Midwestern mentalities. Its almost tangible cultural history still seemed poised to support a regeneration, and it was home to a bevy of respectable colleges and universities that could sustain a real educational and economic renaissance.

But the city—like the youth about whom we cared most and whose lives we relate in this text—seemed to remain mired in the idea of its potential rather than the enactment of this promise. And the community's rejection of its schools seemed like a recycled reactionary act. Community members did not know what they believed would help their children survive and achieve, but they knew the schools were not the solution.

Yet sadly, it took a near tragedy for us to begin to really pay attention to Cleveland's decades-old dropout statistics, the grander community relationship to school these numbers represented, and the fact that we should be addressing these realities through our teaching. On an October school day in 2000, the gymnasium roof at a just twenty-year-old Cleveland high school collapsed onto the floor below, continuing on into the basement where student athletes were running on the indoor track. Miraculously, no one was seriously hurt in this accident, but what had been a strangely quiet tension surrounding the city's schools suddenly erupted.

While the unexpected breakdown of a school building's two-decade-old structure shined an intense but questionably effective spotlight on how such a crisis might have been averted, this event planted a seed of an inquiry in us that has bloomed over the past ten years. Why—when the walls of their schools were literally crumbling around them or when their communities seemed not to care about their academic achievement—would students in Cleveland's schools continue to show up every day? This question might be asked—perhaps *should* be posed—in every one of our nation's urban centers, in every one of its increasingly diverse communities, and in every neighborhood where dropout rates remain high or are rising. Even in those where the school buildings are not in danger of collapsing.

Of course, the answers to this most basic query are tremendously complicated, and the reality is that city youths' stays in school often are frustratingly short-lived. But this question about what school actually means to urban young adults—and the process of asking these young people this inquiry in a way that might engage them both immediately and long term with school and its promise—have become our most effective and important pedagogical method, which we share in the remainder of this book. Of course, this question is relevant not just to Cleveland, its schools, and their students but also to young people, community members, teachers, and educational institutions throughout our nation—in any context where the social contract of schooling appears to be damaged or broken.

Urgent public outcries from youth, community members, and politicians followed the collapse of the East High School gymnasium roof in 2000. We witnessed a short-lived rally around the schools, which resulted in the eventual passing of a $100 million bond issue to remake at least the physical structures in which at that time approximately fifty thousand children and young adults gathered each day. But almost fifteen years later, not much appears to have changed in terms of either the schools' buildings or the city's relationship with the very institution of public education, other than the dwindling enrollment that echoes reduced involvement. Any improvements appear only in pockets, evidence of the lack of school funding equity across very different neighborhoods for which so many school administrators and politicians intensely argued and planned.

Dropout rates remain essentially the same, charter schools are only slightly better regulated, student achievement by any measure is at best nominally improved, and the school population has shrunk to just over thirty-five thousand children and youth. More than twenty-five school buildings have been closed in the past decade, while others have been refurbished and rebuilt, and the district is on its fourth CEO. Each new leadership team attempts seemingly every reform idea it can generate—like throwing pasta against a wall, trying to see what sticks—in an effort to turn the tide of decades of school failure. These "reforms" now include the creation of district-sponsored, pseudo-charter schools that continue to conflate school *choice* with school *quality*. But, as in too many communities like Cleveland around the country, we still seem to be waiting for the sky—or at least the ceiling—to fall.

Our Schools and Our Stories

"I Learned Not to Give Up"

This is Mr. Fenner, my math teacher. Sometimes his class is hard and you have to pay attention or you won't get it. I also struggled in math, but when I came to high school I started to pay attention. In middle school I just gave up. In 9th grade I was able to go to John Carroll University for a math competition. In middle school my friends distracted me, and I was always laughing, over stupid things. My friends who were around me always joked a lot. I guess this was my way of getting attention. I knew my success had to start in high school, and if I wanted to go to college, I had to really buckle down. Mr. Fenner is always there when we have questions. He always shows us different ways of doing problems. He gives us homework, but it helps us. He shows how to do homework so that we'll know what to do when we get to the test. I learned not to give up. I knew that I could do the math work if I put my mind to it. It takes determination. I'm determined to go to college. —Monique

Monique was another tenth-grader in a language arts class when we first met her and she began to work with the Through Students' Eyes project. While she was in this honors English class, Monique began to engage with writing tasks when we put our image-based inquiries into her relationship to school at the center of our lessons, and when we took the risk to ask her to show and tell us why she came to school and what helped and hindered her attendance and success.

Monique and her story have come to represent our very personal motivations behind the work of TSE and its focus on our cities—on increasingly diverse suburban and ex-urban centers around the United States, on schools filled with too often disenfranchised young people who look nothing like us, and, most importantly, on youths' perspectives on these institutions. She reminds us about the broader public's perceptions of our schools, and she confirms what the efforts of individual and small groups of teachers—like Mr. Fenner, who she depicted standing in a shadowy classroom, teaching from an overhead projector—might mean for engaging today's youth with our foundational educational institutions.

As we shared earlier in this chapter, when we first started to work with Rhodes High School on Cleveland's southwest side in 2000, the school was an educational, institutional beacon in the night. While its building was in the same decrepit condition as virtually every Cleveland school—with broken windows, missing ceiling tiles, graffiti-covered walls inside and out, and often even holes in some classroom partitions—it had clearly been built in a time when the district and city were in much better financial shape. The school's population did not appear to be much different than most of its Cleveland counterparts—made up of a racially and ethnically diverse group of youth, almost all of whom were working class or working poor.

While Rhodes was admired districtwide for the fact that it appeared to be functioning well, at least in the most rudimentary sense, its students still faced poverty, transience, and an average high school graduation rate of between 60 and 70 percent.

While Rhodes was familiar to us—we had both been teaching and living in cities for most of our adult lives at that point—it suddenly seemed especially important that we acknowledge that we were not from the same communities as our students, and that we must work extra hard to learn and understand their own and their families' personal and school stories. Yet while our life and professional experiences might seem dramatically different from those of our students, they still deeply inform our work with TSE and our efforts to help our diverse, urban students make sense of and appreciate school.

Kristien grew up outside of Chicago but attended high school in rural Indiana. He not only made it through high school, but, in retrospect, he valued virtually every step of his own schooling process. He often shares his school history with our TSE students and, perhaps even more importantly, he recounts the schooling story of his father in elaborate detail. While his dad is long-since retired, his schooling experiences strangely mirror those of the city youth with whom we work: he just made it through high school, and he has never been able to achieve any significant worldly success, at least not in his own eyes. He is an amazingly talented individual, but his gifts are known mostly by his kids, all of whom idolize him.

While his mom and dad never preached about school, Kristien still knew what achievement in school meant: it was a promise of hope and perhaps the only avenue he had to realize the potential that remains just that in his father. After fifteen years as an English teacher in Seattle, Chicago, and Indiana, Kristien arrived in Cleveland to start his first job as a professor of literacy education at Cleveland State University just months before the East High School gym roof collapse. As a new academic but long-time city resident and teacher, he thought that perhaps he was witnessing the explosive rebirth of a community's appreciation for its schools.

Like Kristien, Jim is also a veteran city English teacher, but he is also what we recognize as a classic example of irony. He barely graduated from an inner-ring Cleveland high school, and, as we noted earlier in this chapter, his cumulative grade point average as a senior was just above 1.6. He remembers receiving a phone call at home the day before his high school commencement letting him know that, in fact, he *would* be able to walk the stage with his peers the next day.

Jim's poor school performance was not due to substandard intelligence: like so many of our students today, and like Kristien's dad, he just did not comprehend the importance of education in his youth, at the time when he had such ready access to schooling opportunities. He was labeled the product of a lazy, father-absent family, and he failed two math classes and two English classes, one of them being sophomore English. Here's the irony: he now *teaches* sophomore English in another urban high school where we regularly implement our project. Jim also shares his personal story of high school with his students and the youth in the TSE project because he wants them to know how much time—and for that matter, money—he wasted by not taking advantage of high school.

We have shared additional information about our personal and professional paths into this project in the Preface to this text. Maybe it is because our lives and schooling experiences often do not parallel those of the youth with whom we are working that we are very intentional about sharing our own stories with our students. We want them to appreciate that even teachers and college professors do not always "get" school and can find school a troubling and irrelevant institution. That we are willing to question its nature and structures with the same vigor that we are asking them to do, so that ultimately we can partner—teachers, students, community members, all of us—to make it what it should be: a place where, as Monique, suggests, we learn never to give up.

3

The Foundations of Our Practices

FIGURE 3.1

"My Name Is Short"

What makes me unsuccessful in school is language. . . . My name has caused me many problems in America. In Sri Lanka, my name is short and everyone can pronounce it. However, in America, my name is long and difficult to pronounce so nobody can say it correctly. When I do an assignment for class, I have to make sure there is a space provided for my name. Otherwise I need to add a space so people will know it is my name and not just a word. . . . Sometimes I cannot understand what Americans are talking about because there are a lot of differences between American English and British English. I have to use American English. Otherwise, Americans won't understand me . . . ."Neighbor" in America is "neighbour" in British English. This makes me confused and crazy. Another problem is reading in English. Sometimes the teacher just says, "Read the book." I can read, but I cannot understand everything I read. Having a list of definitions to words I don't understand would help me read better. In math, I don't know the names of the expressions and the different names associated with the different types of math. English is hard and can make me unsuccessful in school. —Anuruddha

Anuruddha was an eighth-grade student in the classroom of one of the extraordinary teachers with whom we have worked with Through Students' Eyes over the past decade. He was someone who even the most worldly among us could not help but notice. He was very tall for his age and appeared several years older than virtually all of his classmates. He was clearly of Middle Eastern descent in a community that was still dealing with—maybe even reeling from—what seemed like an instantaneous evolution in its demographics.

Without a single sign of the impending shift, the region had changed from rural, White, relatively wealthy Virginia farming sections of three counties to an ex-urban collection of bedroom neighborhoods. From a series of distinct, small communities it now appeared to be one larger district whose borders were blurred by the upsurge in Central American immigrants who were employed by a burgeoning service sector. Yet even in now midsized towns that were more racially and ethnically diverse than ever before in their histories, Anuruddha stood out.

It did not take long for us to appreciate that he was a highly intelligent young man with a bit of a cosmopolitan awareness. Every interaction we had with Anuruddha suggested that he was a dedicated student and fluent in English. But as his image and reflection above suggest, in his short time in the United States he had already come to a profound, troubling understanding of the realities of school. He recognized, and he was able to articulate, that his school-related English activities called less for his intelligence or diligence and more for his ability to navigate expectations that were more foreign to him than the language he thought he knew.

Anuruddha was struggling in many of his classes not because of a lack of academic or intellectual curiosity, or as the result of his family's absence of interest in his school success, or even because of the culturally foreign content or the unique schooling institution to which he had only recently been introduced. Rather, as he conveyed with his picture and writing above, he was having difficulty primarily because his teachers—reasonably, it seemed—assumed that he would understand all of what they considered the most basic and obvious structures of school. Instead of explaining ostensibly transparent procedures like how to fill in his unusually long name in a limited number of spaces on a standardized test cover sheet or providing him with guidance with very necessary context clues for reading his textbooks, his teachers focused on the lowest common monitoring denominator of appearances. He looked as if he knew what he was doing, and he looked as if he *should* know what he was doing, so they did not bother to provide the support for which he was increasingly desperate.

What might have seemed like a tremendously complex set of factors that were impeding Anuruddha's and many of his peers' success was actually a fairly simple set of conditions. Eventually, we worked closely enough with him and other young people in our diverse classrooms (which included even those who had been born in the United States and attended American schools their entire lives) to recognize that it was these systems that were hindering much of their school achievement. And the result was that our students wrote quantifiably more, and more proficiently, than ever before.

This apparent contradiction—when something appears complicated but upon closer examination is actually quite simple—is a perfect metaphor for the Through Students' Eyes photovoice method. But of course, these techniques do not exist in a vacuum; they rely on a host of other ideas, teaching practices, and assumptions. In this chapter we explore these foundations of our photovoice and visual sociology strategies.

Out of something akin to a teaching desperation, we have considered a wide range of fields and pedagogies to weave together the methods on which we now rely. We are, first and foremost, veteran English teachers committed to serving youth who are too often disengaged from not only our writing activities but also from school in general. We are also like so many other teachers in similarly intensified circumstances: as experienced, intelligent, and well intentioned as we might be, too often we are grasping at those proverbial straws when it comes to finding the best writing instruction methods to serve our students.

Fortunately, we have identified not only the rich range of strategies we discuss throughout this book but also notions that give us foundations for our practices—bases that too often teachers do not have when they are selecting and crafting their pedagogies. These underpinnings include notions of cultural relevance, the concept of multimodal literacy, research on student voice, and visually oriented and Youth Participatory Action Research (YPAR) methods. We also look to teaching practices and scholarship that consider students' perspectives and voices as key sources of information about schools, teaching, and curricula. Combined, these form a set of project-based teaching and research practices that might serve our most diverse and disenfranchised students and simultaneously promote their own and our understanding of what school *might* mean and *actually* means—in large part by promoting diverse youths' writing development.

Culture and Relevance

"Blur Baby Blur"

The blurry shade of soft beautiful light grips the background of the crimson red paint of the walls. Kinda ironic, right? I have a tendency at times to over-exaggerate simple and mundane details to where they are a distinct distortion. Basically I can make a simple story of walking down the hallway and tripping halfway down into an epic fantasy with a villain and a temptress distracting from my goal. This scene I feel (at least to me) is an extension of that. This is what prevents me from being successful. My utter obsession with everything around me usually sets me off topic or project. It takes a collection and floods of endless thought just to accomplish a task. Everything in my head is often abstract and almost impossible to relate. I just feel like I am floating around, never really on the ground. —Joseph

Joseph was an understated presence in Jim's sophomore English class at Euclid High School the year we also worked with him in the photovoice project. He was affable, polite, and very well spoken. A student of multiple racial origins, Joe was explicitly aware of the effect his speech (many of his classmates would have described it as unusually proper) had on his peers. Yet standing out in this way did not seem to faze him. He was just as likely to launch into a discussion of the portrayal of race in the *Star Wars* films as he was to analyze Holden Caulfield's motivation in *Catcher in the Rye*.

On the surface, Joe was in no way a typical urban high school student. He was a more progressive thinker and more willing to consider big ideas than many of his peers, as evidenced by the shadowy image of a lamp in his bedroom that he described with the almost poetic reflection above. And while he often described himself to us as "awkward," he was clearly comfortable in that inelegance and even seemed to embrace it. He never apologized for his apparent lack of grace as if it were a liability. Rather, he shocked us with his self-acceptance of his somewhat gawky manner, as if it were just a part of him. As fellow geeks, we appreciated that in Joe.

Still, Joe also carried himself in a way that broadcast an overall lack of self-assurance, as a young man who clearly wanted to fly under the social radar. Thus, it was no great surprise to us when Joe visited New York City on a family trip over the following summer that he found a man wearing a *Star Wars* Boba Fett mask playing an accordion and documented the unusual scene with his digital camera. This was Joe's kind of guy: someone quietly, but decisively, doing his own thing.

The school year after Joe participated in TSE, Jim's principal came to us with a story of his attendance at the previous night's Parent-Teacher Association (PTA) meeting, where Joe's mom had been present. She had raved about how the project had brought Joe out of his shell and given him a heightened sense of confidence—to the point that, as Joe's mom tearfully announced, Joe was then even considering modeling as a career path. We were stunned: Joe had been one of those students who we assumed did not need—and likely would not benefit from—any of the alternative approaches we were sharing with TSE.

Joe had already found his place within, or made peace with, the culture of school. He was achieving a respectable level of academic success. He appeared to be on his way to a reasonable range of post–high school prospects. But he reminded us that interventions that rely on alternative pedagogies and curricula—particularly ones that honor our students' cultures and literacies—may be good for *all* youth. Even those who we assume are on a personal and professional life path that suggests future success, even toward achievements that are less meaningful than they desire: perhaps *all* of our students need the positive interruptions in how their cultures and literacies are appreciated in our classrooms that projects like TSE provide.

Thus, one of the primary foundations of our photo-based work with youth is the notion of "culturally relevant pedagogy" (CRP), which is likely best characterized as a curricular theory. We arrived at CRP in an authentic way: through interactions with youth like Joe we began to appreciate that we *had* to consider students' cultures in our English and writing content and pedagogies. Popularized in the last two decades primarily through the work of Gloria Ladson-Billings and Geneva Gay, CRP adds an explicit focus on "culture" as a core element of any curriculum. A CRP orientation contradicts that "deficit" model introduced in chapter 1, which suggests that the cause of a student's underachievement in or disenfranchisement from school rests within the individual rather than in her/his environment, historical circumstances, school curricula, or teachers' pedagogies.

While often a nebulous concept, a culturally relevant approach recognizes education as neither politically nor culturally neutral, calling on educators to help students challenge the current social order. CRP has long focused on teacher traits and the curricula teachers implement, mindful of the cultural dimensions that affect student learning (Esposito and Swain 2009). Working with youth who too often were entrenched in relationships to school and to our English and writing curriculum that led to their almost automatic rejections of these, we were determined to find a pedagogical orientation that began with students contesting this school social order.

Culturally relevant pedagogy concentrates on addressing cultural mismatches between components of students' lives and school in an effort to facilitate children's and youths' academic success while building teachers' cultural competence (Boutte and Hill 2006). As well, CRP acknowledges that many students need assistance developing alternative and more positive stories of school—what scholars sometimes call "counternarratives" about their cultures, their academic abilities, and the relationships between these (May and Sleeter 2010; Villegas and Lucas 2007). Such counternarratives might result from youths who have the opportunity to share their experiences as part of the curriculum or teachers who make diverse adolescents' life events the very content of the curriculum. These ideas resonated with and supported our instincts to explicitly appeal to young adults' perspectives on school, both as a sign of respect for our students and their cultures and so that we could consider their points of view in our teaching.

We also appreciated the concept of CRP because it has proven to empower ethnically diverse youth and adolescents from underresourced communities who struggle to engage with school due to societal perceptions of their deficiencies (Gay 2010; Ladson-Billings 2009). CRP assumes that to address the challenges faced by marginalized and minority youth, educators must reorient "the onus of responsibility for student academic and behavioral failure away from the student and instead look at the educator, the curricula, the school and the cultural mismatch between all three" (Journell and Castro 2011, 11). Culturally relevant pedagogies enhance youths' positive ethnic identities and help them challenge the racism that numerous critics note stubbornly permeates the culture of US schools (Hanley and Noblit 2009; Seidl 2007).

Literacy—and "Literacies"

"The Glue in My Life"

Without my grandma I would not be a senior in high school. I would not be at school every day trying to complete all of my assignments. I wouldn't be filing for financial aid or even scouting for colleges. My grandma is the glue in my life. If it was not for her I wouldn't be as together as I am. I would just be another teenager going nowhere. She has pushed me to succeed in life. She tells me that I should just suck it up and go on, that even if sometimes I think I can't I will come out on top. She is the best support system you could ever have. —Amanda

Amanda photographed her grandmother at the local diner she managed and where Amanda worked. She described the role her grandma played in her life and schooling—someone about and for whom we might ask young women and men to write. Amanda's grandmother encouraged her literacy achievement, and she recognized Amanda for the writing accomplishments with which we were naturally concerned as English teachers. And she "sweated the details" when it came to completing English homework, a financial aid application, or writing a college essay.

Amanda clearly considered her grandmother, with whom she lived and worked, as a key support for her success in school. At the time Amanda took this picture, she was close to finishing high school, a student in Jim's video production course at Lincoln-West High School. In the nearly ten years since, we have tried to keep in touch with Amanda, watched as she married her high school sweetheart, had a child, and lost her husband in an accident caused by a drunk driver. Amanda has become the glue in her own daughter's life, completing college and working to provide a life she and her husband would want, and the kind that her grandmother afforded her in what most would describe as a "nontraditional" family structure.

Amanda's writing showed us that a directly responsible, "traditional" mother and father were not always essential to the school and writing success we so often attribute to a "good" home life. In fact, as Amanda proved later in her own life as a too-young widow, and as Amanda's grandmother proved for her, she sometimes had to adopt a firm mind-set—as she describes it, the ability to "suck it up and go on"—in spite of the traumas of real life. This frame helped Amanda deal not only with the challenges of a community in which school was largely considered unimportant but also with the unimaginable nightmare of losing her partner, Sean, in a tragedy.

As English teachers and teacher educators, we are naturally interested in the notion of "literacy"—defined as the "quality or state of being literate, especially the ability to read and write." And as veteran teachers committed to our own and our students' continued growth, we certainly appeal to many educators and scholars for theories, ideas, and pedagogies that might best serve our increasingly diverse students and promote their reading and writing and speaking and listening achievement. We, like so many teachers around the United States and in most diverse educational settings, had struggled with the deficit perspective we recognized our schools, curricula, and assessment practices appeared to have on our students' general abilities and particularly their writing proficiency. Of course, teachers and schools never explicitly frame children in this deficit manner, but most pedagogical approaches still seemed to assume that our students must be "fixed" by the traditional school and literacy content on which teachers rely.

Thus, the concept of "literacy" that serves as a key foundation of our Through Students' Eyes project work is actually a different one, which might be defined as a "person's knowledge of a particular subject or field." While our goal is our students' enhanced, positive relationships to school and writing, the way that we best promote youths' traditional literacy success is by first recognizing that they are "literate" in many things other than just school subjects. They demonstrate knowledge of, capacities in, and vast experience that our schools and even our English classes might not traditionally appreciate. By this definition, a "literacy" is not necessarily a positive thing—it's just a *thing*.

The connections between this expanded notion of "literacy" and the concept of "cultural relevance" on which we rely are significant. Many examples of research on cultural relevance exist (e.g., Bondy, Ross, Gallingane, and Hambacher 2007; Duncan-Andrade 2006) but remain on the fringes of mainstream concepts of literacy (Esposito and Swain 2009). Instances of the merging of cultural relevance and literacy education depict the integration of critical perspectives into language arts instruction (Edwards, Dandridge, McMillon, and Pleasants 2001; Greene and Abt-Perkins 2003; Morrell 2007). We sought expanded notions of "literacy" that might help us better serve our diverse and too often disenfranchised students.

We feel fortunate that more recently progressive scholars, teachers, and teacher educators have explored and documented broader notions of literacy that recognize that our students have a much wider range of "literacies" and are fluent in languages and with texts that too often are not appreciated by our schools. Literacy educators and researchers have provided not just alternative theoretical lenses on literacy but also numerous examples of the teaching and assessment practices through which students' literacy capacities might be viewed, supported, and engaged by our assignments and assessments. "Literacy" now is understood as a "new" and "multimodal" activity (Alvermann and Strickland 2004; Kress and Van Leeuwen 2006; Moje et al. 2008). In fact, *every* person possesses a literacy capacity—or, in fact, a range of "literacies." And of course, this recognition runs counter to that more traditional "deficit model" perspective.

These educators and thinkers argue, too, that the forms and content of these capacities should be honored and considered foundational to both the media through which we educate youth and the products we regard as evidence of their learning. The texts and forms with which young people are now recognized as being literate include visual, electronic, musical, and cultural structures and media (Christenbury, Bomer, and Smagorinsky 2009; Leu, Kinzer, Coiro, and Cammack 2004). Relying on an expanded set of texts, such as visual media and texts drawn from students' communities, allows young people who are not proficient with traditional school texts to recognize themselves and be recognized by their teachers as fluent, capable, proficient, and *literate*.

Unfortunately, while numerous investigators have demonstrated how literacy educators might integrate these broader notions and examples of literacy into their pedagogies (Lankshear and Knobel 2006; Morrell 2007), these considerations remain the exception for most classroom teachers (Van Horn 2008; Williams 2008; Zenkov 2009). They also are finding favor in fewer teachers' practices as high-stakes testing pressures narrow the curriculum (Herrington, Hodgson, and Moran 2009). These high-stakes assessments, which rely solely on traditional, narrow notions of literacy and texts, are increasingly thrust upon "failing" schools and students as the only acceptable evidence of their academic abilities.

Even more important, students' literacy development plays a primary role in their decisions to remain in or drop out of school (Smyth 2007). Numerous studies have documented how schools' curricular responses to some populations' low traditional literacy rates contribute to overall school disengagement (Lan and Lanthier 2003; Samuelson 2004; Zenkov and Harmon, 2009). This broad notion of literacy offered the recognition that, without necessarily being conscious of our students' "literacies," many teachers know that students are capable of so much more than school often allows.

As optimistic and as committed to social justice as most teachers and teacher educators are, we were hungry for a lens on literacy and our teaching—and methods to match—that would allow us to appreciate and access these abilities, one that would not judge the literacies our students have but would honor the fact that they are knowledgeable about many subjects. By revering them in this way, perhaps we might begin to build a bridge back to school and our writing instruction for them. Or, to honor Amanda's metaphor: we might be the glue in their school and writing lives.

Student Voice

FIGURE 3.2

"School Is A Struggle"

This photo can be used to explain an obstacle to my success in school. In this photo it shows the gate over the school welcome sign. This picture makes me feel like I'm trapped in a jail cell with no hopes of escaping in the near future. It is extremely hard to go to school each day worrying about people and their drama. If I could eliminate people from school it would be perfect. Teachers add to the drama in school when they bring their home life with them. They are always preaching, "Check your attitude at the door!" when they don't even do it themselves. School is ten times harder when a disrespectful teacher triggers you purposely because they know you will say something back. School, especially high school, is portrayed to be something exciting and memorable, instead it is memorable for all the wrong reasons. Most of the time the memories that stay with us are the ones where we feel alone in the world or when no one cares about you or what you represent. Great success is achieved when high school is completed, but the journey is nowhere near over in life. —Ebony

If you had not read Ebony's writing above or seen the accompanying image, you might be tempted to think she was the model student: polite, participating whenever she was called on, and even an occasional volunteer. Ebony presented with the calm demeanor of a mature young adult who knew what she wanted out of life: to be a pediatrician. And what college she planned to attend: The Ohio State University. And what she expected on a day-to-day basis from the people in her life: respect.

We were absolutely shaken by the reflection that Ebony drafted for this particular photograph. Here was a student in the top 5 percent of her class, who was not even remotely struggling to succeed in or out of the classroom. Yet Ebony was someone who in spite of appearing absolutely confident about how to play the "game" of school was a deeply dissatisfied educational consumer.

Ebony was not the kind of adolescent to get pulled into others' disagreements, no matter how juicy such a distraction might be. Through her work as a conflict mediator, she was aware of the pitfalls of her peers' somewhat soap-operatic approach to relationships. To think that teachers might be purposely triggering her into some sort of confrontation was almost unbelievable to us.

But we knew Ebony well and trusted her as much as any student we had encountered. Her instinct was to play the school dynamic from a distance. She already did not seem bothered by the fact that even she—one of the most successful members of her graduating class—would eventually depart with a shortage of fond memories.

As public schools are redefined and appear to be under attack by seemingly every policy and commercial entity, not to mention from virtually every set of their traditional supporters and constituents, teachers can ill afford to have any young person—perhaps especially students like Ebony—dismissing school for any reason, particularly not for reasons that are under educators' control: the lack of professionalism of our teacher colleagues. Rather, we should aim to have all of our students—again, perhaps particularly youths like Ebony—do cartwheels of joy as they leave our care.

As much as it pained us to read Ebony's laments about her teacher's behavior and to talk through other elements of school that engender similar frustration or disgust, we appreciated that we needed to hear these complaints and concerns. It became obvious—Ebony told us as much—that our inquiries into her perspective helped her, if only momentarily, to like school and to want to engage with us and this institution just a little bit more. This consideration of youths' points of view is another of the key elements of the Through Students' Eyes process, and one that we are grateful is being replicated in projects around the United States.

The reality is that the voices of diverse city youth have long been almost nonexistent in public and policy debates about schools and teachers' practices (Doda and Knowles 2008; Fine, Torre, Burns, and Payne 2007). Fortunately, the past decade has produced considerable literature on youths' perspectives on school (Cook-Sather 2009; Schmakel 2008; Yonezawa and Jones 2009). Research and curricular projects have explored how young adults can serve as authentic informants about how school structures might better suit their needs (Ayala and Galletta 2009; DeFur and Korinek 2009; Mitra and Gross 2009; Rudduck 2007; Stricklan, Keat, and Marinak 2010; Thiessen 2007).

These studies have helped us to understand factors related to the success and failure of these young people in school, in our language arts classes, and with our writing activities (Zenkov 2009). This research has documented how diverse young people long for flexible school schedules, for programs that simultaneously support their own *and* their families' achievement, and for smaller classes that keep youth from getting lost in large high schools. And a considerable body of these reports has revealed how *all* youth—even those students who otherwise appear to have given up on school—simply long to be involved in school restructuring efforts (Jurkowski 2008; Rubin 2007; Shah and Mediratta 2008).

Methods for "Seeing" School

"Go to a Friend's House"

To me the purpose of school is to socialize with my friends. I don't like to do work in school because sometimes it is too hard for me. For example, I don't understand some things in social studies, especially when the teacher asks me to complete a project. The ideas are difficult for me to understand. I get bad grades because I don't come to school every day. I would rather skip school and go to a friend's house than come work hard in school. I get frustrated because the work is too hard and I don't understand it. When I come to school, I want to have fun with my friends because learning is too hard. But I know I need to go to school to learn so that I can graduate and get a good job. —Julio

Julio was an eighth-grader in a language arts class for English-language learn-ers when we introduced him to our photo-elicitation project. He was a bright young man who playfully engaged with us, his teachers, and other caring adults in his classroom. Sadly, he often struggled to find reasons to positively participate in school, to complete our reading and writing assignments, and to demonstrate the English proficiency he needed to be successful in school and beyond.

Julio was a somewhat erratic participant during the first month while we worked with him on the project. He only occasionally took pictures. While he talked at length about the promise of the project and his grand ideas for pictures he might take, he rarely showed himself or us that he was able to participate fully and consider the questions of our project in a significant way. His stance toward the project shifted dramatically one day, though, when Kristien sat with him and reviewed his images.

Julio drafted the above paragraph accompanying his photograph—it seemed like an innocuous picture of two teachers in an affectionate pose with two students—almost verbatim on that day, but he chose this image only after Kristien showed great interest in his photographs and engaged him in lengthy conversations about each one. We watched Julio's investment in the project, its processes, and his writing grow almost minute by minute over the course of an hour, through Kristien's sincere curiosity in his photographic work and the stories behind them. Julio seemed to think that we would assume that his attraction to interacting with his peers was a stereotypically negative activity for youth. But through Kristien's careful facilitation of the elicitation process, we began to appreciate the complexity of the distractions our students wanted us to consider.

When we appeal to these photovoice methods that begin with young adults' photographs rather than more traditional school literacy practices, our stu-dents are not only able to grow as writers and engage as students, but they can also provide poignant insights into the realities of what is and is not working in our schools. The multimodal literacy and student voice practices on which we rely come together quite neatly under Youth Participatory Action Research (YPAR) traditions (Kemmis and McTaggart 2000; McIntyre 2008). Like the Through Students' Eyes projects, YPAR is conducted within a participatory community with the goal of addressing an area of concern and identifying ac-tions that improve the quality and equity of outcomes (Mediratta, Shah, and

McAlister 2009). YPAR amplifies diverse youth voices, particularly around issues of educational justice (Carlo et al. 2005; Torre 2005; Zeller-Berkman 2007).

Echoing our photovoice activities, YPAR researchers also increasingly use visual tools (K. Marquez-Zenkov, Harmon, van Lier, and M. Marquez-Zenkov 2007; Mitchell et al. 2005; Wilson et al. 2007). When applied to examinations of youths' perspectives on notions of curricular relevance, image-based tools are among the most accessible to today's adolescents (Graziano 2011; Streng et al. 2004). Visual texts motivate youth to engage in reading and writing tasks, promote their sense of literacy efficacy (Marquez-Zenkov and Harmon 2007; Zenkov and Harmon 2009), and allow them to analyze classroom realities.

Researchers have detailed how youths' proficiency with a range of untraditional texts—including visual media and photographic images—provides the groundwork for teaching methods and curricula that advance adolescents' appreciation for traditional literacy activities and new angles on their connections to school (Hibbing and Rankin-Erickson 2003; Kroeger et al. 2004; Marquez-Zenkov 2007; Moje et al. 2008). For example, by beginning lessons with these visual tools, which students typically do not perceive as "school" texts, young people have been able to forget and see past their self-perceptions and their characterizations as "struggling" readers, writers, and students (Streng et al. 2004).

Educators and scholars increasingly use "photo elicitation" techniques to access adolescents' insights that language-centered methods cannot (Raggl and Schratz 2004). These visually based methods provide our multimodally literate young people with tools with which they are already fluent, using them to bridge to language rather than beginning with traditional literacy forms. The visual arts draw on and develop students' abilities to observe, envision, and explore untraditional ideas and, simultaneously, to reflect on that process. These media also help students engage in metacognition and the skills involved with stepping back from—and being able to describe and interpret—one's experiences, rather than simply *having* experiences (Hetland, Winner, Veenema, and Sheridan 2007).

Relevant to our project is the fact that, while many studies of youths' perceptions of school have been language-focused inquiries, some of these research efforts have looked to the technology-oriented and visually oriented media with which youth are familiar. We have witnessed time and again how our middle school and high school students are considerably more comfortable with visually oriented and technology-oriented tools than are our preservice teachers. Today's young people are simply more *literate* in these tools. Young adults, we find, generally are better able to illustrate concepts with images than most teachers. Yet few future teachers recognize that their students are *more* literate than they are in some capacity, primarily because of a digital generation gap. That is, most preservice teachers are completing preparation programs under the guidance of very veteran university faculty and school-based mentors who are reluctant digital migrants, who simply do not have the capacity to serve as the models they need.

This project and the pedagogical approach it represents also allow young adults to engage as proficient writers, to own the adultlike tasks of questioning the social contract of schooling, and to have their responses validated as contributions to authentic discussions of the purposes of school. These adolescents' engagement with literacy and life skills has been both a product and a mechanism of this project—outcomes and devices that these culturally relevant, broad literacy-based, student voice-oriented, and visually-driven participatory action research activities readily promote—ones through which our diverse youth may be best able to show us what they already know about *and* what they would like to see in our schools.

4

Picturing a Writing Process

FIGURE 4.1

"Uphill All the Time"

This is a photograph of the hill I walk up and down every day to get to and from work. I started working full time at the zoo to help out my family. I don't make a lot, but what I do make helps pay for my dad's prescriptions and allows me to take care of my own expenses so my family does not have to worry about me. Every day when I come home from work I walk uphill, and I feel like I'm walking uphill all the time. —Lindsay

Lindsay was a junior at Rhodes High School when we met her. She and her best friend Kayla were inseparable, highly intelligent, always dressed in stereotypical gothic garb, and were absolutely unforgiving of teachers who did not challenge them. While neither young woman came from a family where school success or even high school graduation was the norm, they both recognized that achieving in school—and, by extension, in their English class and with our writing assignments—were perhaps the only means they had to forge better lives. Lindsay worked with us on the Through Students' Eyes (TSE) project with a religious consistency, but she maintained a reserved, perhaps skeptical, composure in seemingly every interaction with us. Still, she clearly recognized something of an opportunity in the project, and she revealed her devotion to it by taking and writing about photographs regularly.

Lindsay's images and the ideas she shared through these visuals were among the most carefully considered we have encountered from the more than eight hundred youth with whom we have conducted TSE over the past ten years, but they never seemed staged or clichéd. Once she trusted us, she was hungry to share the realities that she was encountering in her life outside of school. She offered the photograph and drafted the writing above with a laserlike intentionality. And she did so with an apparent cognizance of what she thought her teachers needed to know and how school (including our English classes and our writing activities) might be organized differently in order to serve her better. Lindsay longed for school structures and schedules that would support her family's health care and other daily life needs, or at least allow her and her peers to do so, and thus enable her and her classmates to focus more on our English class activities and school in general.

While Lindsay is now close to finishing college, she was among the merely 50 percent of students to graduate from this city high school. Stories like Lindsay's are all too common. Over years of teaching in Cleveland's and other communities' diverse and too often impoverished neighborhoods, we have come to recognize that too many of these young women and men are faced with economic, family, and health concerns that keep them and their peers from focusing on school. But as we have noted in earlier chapters, we recognized, too, that we simply do not know enough about these youths' notions of school.

As we discussed in the first two chapters, these dropout—or "pushout"— trends and our students' tenuous relationships to school led us to wonder why these young people would continue even to show up every day to an institution that was clearly on the periphery of relevance for them. Rather than assume that school did and should matter to our students, we began to wonder *if* and *why* it did. That is, we recognized that we owed it to our students to engage in some school soul-searching, in some teacher existential contemplation. We began by asking ourselves and inquiring of our teaching practices just what the purpose of school was. But we soon appreciated that this and other related queries that threw our very professional survival into question needed to be asked of our students.

We did not stop there. The premise of the Through Students' Eyes project is that this question *What is the purpose of school?* might be asked—perhaps *should* be asked—in every community around our nation. Of course, the answers to this most basic query are complex, and the reality is that diverse youths' stays in school often are frustratingly short-lived. But this interrogation of what school actually means to young adults—and the project of asking these young people this question in a way that might engage them both immediately and long term with school and its promise—have become our most effective and important pedagogical methods. Our students have offered rich insights into how we might heal that damaged social contract of schooling and their limited relationships to school.

When we began to work with our students to explore their relationships to formal education, it quickly became clear that they were not at all sure about the purposes of what is arguably our society's most foundational institution. In response to this apparent lack of understanding about school's purposes and value, we developed TSE as an intervention in these disenfranchised youths' schooling and writing lives, through which we now ask youth three seemingly straightforward questions:

1. What is the purpose of or why do you come to school?
2. What helps you to be interested in and/or successful in school?
3. What gets in the way of your interest in and/or your success in school?

But we do not just ask them to answer these questions explicitly and with words. Rather, we call on them to respond to these inquiries with pictures, so that we and many other audiences might better see and be able to respond to what our students believe.

In this chapter, we describe an overview and the general implementation steps of TSE, from the introduction of the project, to youths' own production of images and writings, to the eventual exhibition of their photographs and reflections. We offer accounts of some of the foundational writing instruction principles and methods we have developed through our facilitation of the project, including the practice of Asking First, taking Class Pictures, developing a Class Quiz, and the Community Handshake activity. These strategies are also rooted in notions of Blind Faith and Daily Forgiveness, which support teachers to help students to recognize that the Apparently Mundane Matters.

Asking First: Who Our Students Are and Are Not

"I Know My Brother and He Is Good"

One thing that makes me unsuccessful is my mom. She is always mad with my brother and that makes me get mad, too. She thinks my brother is a gangster but he is not. She always tells him, "Luis, don't talk to those guys." She always asks me if Luis is involved with gangsters. She worries about him. My mom worrying also makes me worry about him. I know my brother and he is good. I always spend time worrying and looking out for him. When my mom asks me questions, I cannot concentrate on my homework. In class, I am thinking about my brother and who he talks to. One thing that makes me unsuccessful is my mom because she thinks my brother is a gangster. —Fernando

Fernando was an eighth-grader in one of the language arts classes with which we worked. He had recently moved from El Salvador with his family to the ex-urban community outside Washington, DC. Classified as a Level Two English Speaker of Other Languages (ESOL) student, he appeared to be almost entirely unmotivated to participate in his daily language arts activities.

Only when we asked him to take photographs that depicted what in his life impeded and promoted his success in school did he show any interest in beginning to write. Eventually he described and illustrated how it was the assumptions that teachers and even members of his family made about his own

and his brother's academic abilities that resulted in what we had previously
believed was an impenetrable indifference to school and writing. Through
these pictures, reflections, and conversations, it became clear that the adults
in Fernando's life and in our school had concluded that he and his brother
had only negative identities as students and writers.

Through these visual and written artifacts and interactions, it also became
apparent that Fernando had embraced this pessimistic perspective on his
writing abilities. Like almost all of the students with whom we have worked
through TSE, he and his brother had encountered few academic successes
since their arrival in our schools. And they, like so many of our English-language learners and other too frequently disenfranchised students, had found
it easier simply to feign apathy toward school rather than to try to counter
these perceptions of their abilities or interests.

Thus, the first step in the Through Students' Eyes process involves teachers recognizing that we most often do not have a complete knowledge of
who our students are and that we very likely never will be able to completely
know them or bridge their and our own very different cultures. Teachers
must get comfortable with the idea that not wholly knowing one's students
or even being able to know them is only truly problematic if we are unaware
of this ignorance or if we do not persist in attempting to know them. Teachers acknowledging this perhaps insurmountable gap in our knowledge of the
youth with whom we work is actually an act of empowerment, for us and
our students. This acknowledgment also takes the form of the opening TSE
questionnaire (see appendix 4.1), which youth should complete early on in
these inquiries into their perspectives on school. We then engage students in
follow-up one-to-one interviews, which provides disenfranchised young people, who are almost universally struggling or frustrated writers, with chances
to compose answers to these questions without actually having to write them.

Too, writing teachers accepting the differences between them and their
students and recognizing their lack of familiarity with these youths' histories
and cultures is actually the first and most important step in formulating ways
to come to know these youth. When teachers adopt this humble, inquisitive,
and curious stance before their students, these young people are very often
shocked into greater engagement in our classes. They are often stunned by the
sincere inquiries into their lives that teachers make, by our efforts to consider
their experiences and interests in our curricula, by the fact that we are looking

to them as the experts on any topic. While TSE looks like a writing curricula, such an instructional approach actually begins with that stance of humility, that recognition that *asking* students about school instantly repositions them and opens up the possibility that they might forge new relationships to this institution and to our writing activities.

This orientation of Asking First plays out in at least one very pragmatic, almost nonsensically simple, everyday manner and practice. While we ask students about their perspectives on school—"asking" writ large—we also "ask first" in more momentary ways. For example, when one of our students had committed one of a seemingly endless array of possible schooling sins— arriving late to class or failing to turn in an assignment or even adopting an adversarial tone—we learned to first *inquire* about what might have been the events that led up to this end.

Such a query temporarily stifled any suggestion that the student was in any way responsible for this schooling transgression. Teachers and students in these situations might have already *known* the answer to the questions of causality and culpability—for example, the student was chatting extra long with friends in the hallway, had just disregarded an assignment, or was frustrated by something else in her or his life and had chosen somewhat passive aggressively to take it out on us. But teachers can begin to change the dynamic of the student's relationship to us and our English curriculum by choosing to be patient, by not stating what seems to be obviously true. By assuming the best, by *asking first*.

The physical stances we take as teachers when we are interacting with youths may be just as important. As often as possible, we ask first while squatting down by a student's desk, on their level, daring to demonstrate the sincerity of our inquiry by not making this momentary exchange fully public and certainly not framed as an accusation or a belittling or blaming. Students' relationships to school and writing are frequently synonymous with their relationships to us. And their openness to considering a new writing task or even to begin to develop a wholly different, potentially positive relationship to writing is often rooted in the momentary but absolutely profound acts of respect that we show them.

Because, really, what do we as teachers have to lose by *asking* our students *first* in such situations? The answer, of course: almost nothing. We are simply taking a chance that doing so might make a student feel a bit safer in our classroom, might shift their attitude and experience just enough that they might give a little bit more effort on a writing task. Or, in Fernando's case, *asking first* might counteract, just a bit, the negative assumptions about him and his brother that his parents had come to habitually make. And to help us—and him—to see the good in him and his brother.

Class Pictures, a Class Quiz, and a Community Handshake

FIGURE 4.2

"Moving"

When I moved is when I started going to high school. Getting to school resulted in a problem of being late and missing out on new things to learn. High school was more than what I had ever imagined. This is where a student finds himself among friends and people who care and want for them to succeed which is what helps you in school. And it is where you start to become more of an adult. In the process of this you change from all the things you had done before you moved, such as friends or your daily duties. School and life is like a jungle where when you are moved from one place to another you must adapt and you experience something new each and every time. The good thing about moving is that you . . . get to experience what you never have experienced before. Moving is all about growing up and maturing using all of what you have learned in school. —Bryon

Bryon was one of the most physically striking individuals with whom we have ever worked—he was a statuesque, young African American man with a huge Afro that he unselfconsciously restyled every day. While he was wonderfully sharp and most often at least half-heartedly engaged in his school and writing activities, he was also a senior repeating the eleventh-grade English class when we met. He was a wise young man who would tell you what's what about school, his peers, and life in general, and yet when we asked him what he would do after he graduated from high school he talked about "these computer schools where you go and you can come out and make, like, $80,000 a year." Somewhere in his schooling we had failed to educate him about the realities of paths to success.

More importantly, like so many of his teachers, we were profoundly challenged to see past Bryon's apparent indifference to his schooling work and his English class activities. Many teachers—and popular media and people in the general public—characterize diverse youth as openly resistant to their academics or even to the basic discipline and routines of our classrooms. But like the majority of our students, Bryon was never openly dismissive of completing his assignments for school or the project. Rather, he always matter-of-factly acknowledged that he had not completed a particular task, without any semblance of what most would assume to be remorse and without any promises that he would work on this task immediately.

Bryon was a perfect representative of the young adults with whom we have worked via the TSE project over the past decade. These youth have included African American, Caucasian, Asian American, and Latino/a young women and men, as well as numerous adolescents whose first language is not English. These students came from our urban and ex-urban communities' most racially, ethnically, and linguistically diverse neighborhoods, which are consistently among the most economically impoverished and where the majority are children of high school dropouts or come from families where school has never been—or at least is not yet—a trusted institution. Students' neighborhoods generally were composed of working-poor families, where native English-speaking ninth-graders average as low as a fifth-grade reading level and where non-native English speakers average a second-grade level. Ultimately, our students' and their families' and communities' disengagement from school suggested that we could not assume that these youth or the adults in their lives would ever know a positive relationship to school.

Because of these adolescents' tenuous relationships to school, us, and our writing curriculum—and because we could never assume that they would even be present or even still living in the same neighborhood the next day or week or month—we have become diligent about facilitating community-building activities with them, particularly at the start of each class or each project implementation. As adult students in university classes or participants in professional development activities, we have often reluctantly received instructors' and facilitators' invitations to engage us in such activities on the first day of any new course or training. And yet, these are the exact sorts of exercises that we implement so religiously and with such constructive effects at the very beginning of the Through Students' Eyes project, and that we know now are foundational to our writing curriculum.

On that first day—even in the first few minutes—of meeting a new group of youth who portray apparent indifference toward school or our English classes, we must immediately demonstrate that we explicitly *know* that they are capable of engaging in ways they, we, their peers, and their other teachers might reasonably believe are not possible. Students almost universally give teachers the benefit of the doubt in those initial hours—then and perhaps *only* then are they willing to tolerate just about any little risk we might ask them to take. The act of assuming that young people possess such potential and the willingness to engage takes at least three forms or three unique activities.

We begin by preparing our opening lesson plans in such detail that we have the time to interact with each and every student at the door as they enter. We recommend that teachers have name tags made up ahead of time so that they can greet youth and hand out these identifiers just as students are crossing the threshold of the classroom or the project site. Intentionally smile at every student, introduce yourself, ask each youth's name, and find their name tag. We ask students to enter the classroom, and then we begin with a naturally motivating, personally relevant project, such as writing about their favorite or their most frustrating experiences in school (see appendix 4.2).

These activities might seem clichéd, but students will almost invariably engage just enough to allow teachers to learn something about them and to enable us to continue our introduction routine with others entering the classroom. By immediately asking adolescents about school, we are communicating that we care about their perspectives and experiences. Teachers may only spend a few minutes after this first class or project session reading the results of the brief personal reflections that are the outcome of this opening day's writing task, but it is hugely beneficial to be careful to take notes on what young people say so that we will be able to use what we learn in future interactions with these youth.

The second activity on which we rely is an extension of these seemingly insignificant introduction strategies. While students are working on that opening writing task, or perhaps while they are completing that questionnaire about their interests and previous school experiences (see appendix 4.2) or even reading a brief high-interest article with which they will stay engaged, it is vital that we introduce them to the central place of photography in our classes and our project.

This is one of those days when it is ideal to have more than one adult in the classroom or the project setting, so that this other adult can help with the basic supervision of students' engagement. While youth are reading or writing, we will pull each student into a corner of the room or into the hallway just outside the classroom and take a couple of pictures of them, explaining that the only people who will see these are us, their teachers, and perhaps their peers in this class.

Again, this is one of those moments when teachers might have to step very far outside of themselves, mustering the energy to introduce this activity with broad smiles and lots of encouragement, and an attitude that the adolescents will participate. We move quickly and respectfully, with reasonable and repeated but brief explanations of our need for these images. Students go with it. Part of the reason they are willing to allow us to take these photographs may be the celebrity culture into which they have been born: who does *not* want to have their pictures taken, to be acknowledged and appreciated in this way?

Incorporating Images in Writing Instruction

Images can be used in thousands of ways to inspire student writing, whether the student took the photograph, the student found it, or the teacher provided it. Consider just a few possibilities:

- Focus on one small detail of an image and create a narrative around that detail.
- Images of people are wonderful for teaching direct and indirect characterization.
- Have students create dialogue between two people in a photo around a central theme.
- Have students respond to news photographs as a means of keeping current on issues.

Photo Fridays is an inactive, but still accessible, Flickr group that encourages uploading and sharing photos that might inspire student writing: http://www.flickr.com/groups/photofridays/.

Teachers can further introduce the importance of visual images in our classes and the complex ways that we will ask youths to take and consider photographs by insisting on taking more than one photograph of each student. Show youths each of these images and again ask for their approval. Presenting these images to them again demonstrates the core respect—for self, for other, for the work—that is imbued in the TSE method.

These momentary interactions allow teachers another brief chance to ask young people about themselves, their school days or years thus far, their weekend or previous evening's or summer activities, or their work, friends, or families. It does not seem to matter what we ask them about; they are again puzzled and somewhat taken aback by our inquiries and our apparently sincere interest in them. But they also appear to appreciate the fact that an adult—a teacher—is giving the distinct impression that she or he cares about some of the details of their lives.

We recommend that teachers then take these photographs and construct a Class Quiz and sometimes Photo Name Tags for the following day, offering students their own personalized picture tag and a contact sheet with pictures of everyone in the class—without any identifying information—and have them fill in as many names as they can as the second day's opening activity.

Photo Name Tags and Contact Sheets

Many image-editing applications, such as Apple's iPhoto, allow users to import photographs and add titles (such as students' names) to the images. One may then print multiple images to a page—a contact sheet—that also displays the image title (e.g., the student's name) right below the image. These can be printed on a color printer and trimmed or on label paper that allows images and titles to be peeled off and adhered to one's shirt.

As elementary an activity as it might seem, such a "quiz" is engaging, meaningful, relatively safe, and somewhat playful even among students who might have known and attended school with each other for years. This succeeding session runs close behind the first day in terms of just how tolerant, willing to take risks, and open students are to beginning to reconsider what are typically resistant or reluctant stances toward school, our class, and our literacy and writing activities.

It turns out that this simple act of being in front of the camera—on that first day of school, when students intentionally, even desperately, dress to make that all-important, start-of-the-new-school-year first impression—becomes a transaction of trust between teachers and young people. It is a risky venture to let a new teacher take your photograph on the first day of school. This technique not only allows students to begin to find some comfort with being in front of the camera in the new ways to which we will introduce them, but it gives them a sense of some of the tensions they might encounter when taking pictures of surprised subjects.

These photographs are another of the foundations for the relationships to school and writing that we hope to help youths develop via this project and these activities. At the end of each project or year, we recommend passing these pictures back to students, who will frequently feign chagrin and note most often subtle but sometimes dramatic changes in their physical features. In this way, images can be powerful tools for helping young people, their peers, and their teachers to become aware of or enhance a consciousness of their growth—which, again, helps them appreciate this place we call school and the writing activities that have been at the core of our interactions.

The final, perhaps the most important, and certainly the riskiest activity—for teachers and students—that we religiously call on teachers to use on the first day of a new class or TSE session is the Community Handshake. The Handshake is a completely transparent—even blatant—attempt at allowing teachers and students to know each other's names and at engaging in a straightforwardly professional and positive manner. Of course, once a student is known by name, they are no longer anonymous, no longer "any student." Any teacher will tell you that the sooner you know a student's name, the sooner you can call on them regularly and build the personalized relationships that are so critical to young adults' willingness to participate in the activities we present.

The Handshake requires the students and teacher to form a circle. Each member of the new community shakes each other's hands four times in total, while making eye contact, smiling at, and saying the name of each person they encounter (see appendix 4.3). The circle rotates in on itself, with each participant shaking each individual's hand first on the outside of the circle and then on the inside. The first time we conduct this activity, each person also states aloud each person's name—again, twice, from the inside and outside of the circle—and the second time through they make mental notes or can silently mouth each person's name, while they are again shaking each participant's hand, making eye contact, and smiling at each other.

After each round of the Community Handshake, we ask the students to discuss why such an activity might be useful, how it might support future constructive interactions as a class or group, and even how it might support their engagement and success as writers. Rather than ask, "Do you like this activity?" or "Do you think teachers should use this activity?" we suggest that teachers ask participants what such an exercise might have to do with the purpose of school or the purpose of this particular class, and, occasionally, how it might actually serve as an impediment to their success in our course or school in general. In this moment, we are nudging youth toward the reflective, metacognitive stance that we will be asking them to take throughout our project and the questions we will be asking them to consider via our photo-elicitation process in the near future. Students are explicitly reminded through this brief discussion that we will be seeking their input on what makes "good" teaching and a "good" school.

For the too-often transient students with whom an increasing number of teachers are working, epitomized by Bryon, the Community Handshake is an opportunity to find a classroom home more quickly than these youths typically would. It allowed teachers to know them, them to know us, and them to know each other in ways that they perhaps had never recognized or appreciated in their classmates or their teachers, even if they had shared classroom space with their peers or other teachers for many previous years. Such a community is, again, foundational to teachers' writing instruction practices and to students' writing engagement and success.

These picture-taking, picture-quizzing, and Community Handshake activities ultimately represent the risks we are going to ask students to take, particularly with forging new, deeper relationships to writing. We tell students repeatedly that we are often going to ask them to try new things for just a few moments here and there. Teachers must model every activity, demonstrating that we will be the most energetic and willing participants in some of the less than "cool" and more than occasionally silly exercises we are nudging them to complete. This stance of invitation is almost uniformly successful, even with youth who might appear "hard" or who have found little success and many conflicts in their English classes, with writing assignments, and with school.

The results of these activities are difficult to describe and gauge, but literally thousands of our students—middle school–, high school–, and university-level folks—have recalled these as some of the most significant of our classes and the TSE project. The activities set the tone, they get us and participants out of our comfort zones, and they begin to build the community that we *all* will need if youth or adults are to engage and grow in the ways we hope, with writing and school. Again, even (perhaps especially) among youth who know each other well—who may be familiar to each other and have established ways of interacting and positioning themselves or being positioned by teachers as having negative writer identities—these intentional opening activities are vital. These are clearly moments to remember what we have come to call the "blind faith" and "daily forgiveness" tenets of our teaching and writing instruction practices.

Daily Forgiveness and Blind Faith

"Piggy Bank"

High school for me is similar to a fashion show. We put on our best clothes every day to walk the halls, and like any great fashion show it takes money. For some getting money is only a matter of asking mom and dad, and others work part time jobs or get gigs cutting grass and shoveling driveways in the winter. But this gets in the way of what we truly come to school for, to learn. I think having to worry about what you're wearing and getting money gets in the way of getting an education. —Amber

Amber shared a photograph of her niece's broken piggy bank to accompany the reflection above. Amber was a highly successful student and an accomplished and engaged writer, and this is why we have chosen her paragraph to illustrate these two key teaching principles. She reminds us that teachers need to be very cautious not to focus too much on youths' "fashions"—their initial appearances and facades and stances toward school and writing.

These may be the most important lessons of this project, and perhaps one of the most significant insights that we try to recall on a daily basis with our students: teachers must never assume that a student's failure to complete a task is evidence that they are not interested in or capable of doing this work. We must be diligent about not reading too much into a youth's facial expression or demeanor when we are interacting around a given task. We must have "blind faith" in students, and we must practice "daily forgiveness" for what might appear to be an inexcusable and incomprehensible inability to engage with these tasks. We are the adults. They are learning how to be.

These young people are calling on teachers, counting on us, and even challenging us to be extraordinarily resilient in the face of their regular rejections of school and our writing activities, as well as with the multigenerational disengagement from school that drove us to ask them to show us just what school is for. While it might seem reasonable—and even necessary, as an intervention strategy—to blame young people for these repeated instances of apparent indifference, they need us, their teachers, to have very short memories. We must forget what we think we know about them at the end of each day, and sometimes at the end of each period, hour, or even minute, so that we can return to them with the same hope with which we started our careers. If we can forget and forgive them in this daily way, they just might show us what school can make possible.

Blind faith and daily forgiveness also mean that teachers' work with youth—whether in our classes or around the activities involved with our project—cannot involve many, if *any*, "shoulds." We might expect that because they are eighth-graders, sophomores, or seniors that they "should" have a particular writing proficiency or "should" have developed a particularly positive relationship to school or at least a mature resignation toward their responsibilities in our classes. But what is the point of these "shoulds"? In fact, these absolutes are irrelevant, futile, and even counterproductive mandates. Instead, we must work to meet students where they are, day after day, forgiving and having faith, encouraging them, until they make even the smallest steps toward engaging and achieving in the ways that, again, we—and they—hope.

Conclusions

In the increasingly narrow assessment contexts in which *all* teachers work, it would be easy to dismiss a set of beliefs, dispositions, or principles as irrelevant to effective writing instruction or to our abilities to promote youths' constructive relationships with school. But the reality is that on many days these beliefs are all that we—teachers and adults who care about adolescents' school and life success—have to rely on. We try to be honest with ourselves and our students about the values we are promoting, and we reinforce for them just how these principles play out in our practices. Perhaps most importantly, we often ask these young people to identify their own beliefs about writing and school, and to share their perspectives on the effectiveness of the pedagogies we use to enact these ideals.

While the practices we have discussed here are deceptively straightforward and can be used in virtually any classroom and with any group of adolescents, the focus of every teacher's efforts must ultimately be on youths' identities as writers and students. Of course, shifts in writer and student identities only occur through the daily, incremental steps in classrooms or project sites like TSE. The core of these strategies is an almost counterintuitive practice of *asking* youth—rather than *telling* them—about the nature of school and our literacy curricula and practices.

Disengaged students may not feel or even be capable of writing and talking about the traditional curricula of our English classes, but they can be very articulate about the experiences they have had and they would like to have in these settings. In a sense, this project and these activities beg the question of what helps youth to be successful writers and students; by assuming that they *should* consider the questions of the purposes, supports for, and impediments to their successful school experiences, we are making the very different and positive conjecture that they *can* do so. As the youth in our project have illustrated through the evidence of this chapter and the other participants' thousands of photographs and reflections, we have virtually nothing to lose and only enhanced school engagement, deeper awareness of the value of school, more positive writer and student identities, and newfound writing achievement to gain from taking such risks and making such grand, positive assumptions.

Ultimately, if teachers are to make writing classrooms safer spaces for young people and their writing achievement, we should explicitly ask students about these sheltering qualities. The best informants for these new and evolving definitions of effective writing instruction may be our diverse students themselves. We are fortunate that we are not alone in engaging youth in such activities and projects; many other educators and community activists are implementing similarly radical, meaningful endeavors with young people.

The search for models of effective writing instruction may not lead to the best examples of such strategies, but may, in fact, be the leading model of such pedagogies. The notions of writing pedagogies that will best serve these students may, then, only be developed and sustained through continued photographic and multimodal explorations of young adults' ideas about school and their places in it. These inquiries call on us to use tools that do not rely on languages or cultures (of English, of school) that these young people do not yet know and to consider media that really may be universally understood (photographs) and to begin with intimate, relationship-based stances in our teaching and research.

Meaningful School Activities

Some other organizations interested in involving youth in meaningful school activities, often relying on photographs, media, and technology:

- Edutopia (www.edutopia.org)
- Freedom Writers Foundation (http://www.freedomwritersfoundation .org)
- Facing History and Ourselves (http://www.facinghistory.org/)
- What Kids Can Do (www.whatkidscando.org)

Appendix 4.1

Through Students' Eyes Project Questionnaire

Name _____ Date _____

Instructions: Do your best to answer the questions below with words, phrases, bullet points, or sentences. After you answer these questions, we will interview you to add more of your ideas.

Purposes

1. What do you believe are the purposes of school? What do you believe will happen as a result of you doing well in school?

   _____

   _____

   _____

   _____

Supports

2. What do you believe helps you to be successful in school? What helps you in and out of school with your academic success?

   _____

   _____

   _____

   _____

Impediments

3. What do you believe gets in the way of your ability to be successful in school? What obstacles exist in and out of school that get in the way of your academic success? What would you like to change in your life so that you could do better in school?

_____

_____

_____

_____

Appendix 4.2

Your Most Favorite and Frustrating Experiences in School

Name _____ Date _____

Instructions: Do your best to answer the questions below with words, phrases, bullet points, or sentences. After you answer these questions, we will interview you to add more of your ideas.

Most Favorite

1. What have been your most favorite experiences in school? What subjects, classes, and teachers have been your most favorite? What experiences in school—NOT in your classes—have been your most favorite?

_____

_____

_____

Most Frustrating

2. What have been your most frustrating experiences in school? What subjects, classes, and teachers have been your most frustrating? What experiences in school—NOT in your classes—have been your most frustrating?

_____

_____

_____

Picturing Your Most Favorite and Most Frustrating Experiences in School

3. If you were to take pictures of your most favorite experiences in school—
   IN and OUT of your classes—what would we see? If you were to take
   pictures of your most frustrating experiences in school—IN and OUT of
   your classes—what would we see?

   _____

   _____

   _____

Appendix 4.3

Community Handshake

The Community Handshake is an activity designed to break down the barriers of anonymity and distance between students. The Handshake allows ALL students to be introduced to each other, and, even more importantly, to engage in a positive interaction, with a smile, physical contact or nod, eye contact, and the use of each others' names. Here's how it works.

1. The Handshake begins by having all members of a class arrange themselves in a standing circle. If a class is too large or the room too small, the class can be broken down into smaller groups and the activity can be repeated with different groups for shorter periods of time over several days.

2. All participants must have name tags, especially if this is a start-of-the-year activity.

3. The teacher starts by moving to the inside of the circle and shaking the hand of each participant while smiling, nodding, saying the name of each person she/he is meeting, and making eye contact.

4. The person next to the teacher—whose hand the teacher shook first—then follows on the inside of the circle, modeling the same handshaking, smiling, and the rest.

5. Eventually the circle folds in on itself, with each person moving to the inside of the circle to shake each person's hand.

6. Each person in the circle eventually makes contact with each other participant twice—once while she/he is on the outside of the circle and once while she/he is on the inside, moving line of people.

7. We often have participants cover up their name tags and try to remember each others' names after this first round. We also debrief about how such an activity might work against the anonymity of typical classrooms.

8. We generally repeat this activity a second time, but without participants saying each others' names. Instead they shake hands, nod, make eye contact, and make mental notes of each others' names.

9. We then cover up our name tags again and try to see who has remembered everyone's names. We then debrief again about how such an activity works to build community in the classroom, as well as discuss modifications (e.g., because some students do not feel safe shaking hands).

5

Picturing Self: Past, Present, and Future

FIGURE 5.1

"Opportunity"

This picture makes me think of how you have one chance at life. You can't miss your one shot. For most people if you mess up or miss your shot, you get a second chance. In my lifestyle it's a hit or miss proposition. That's why I go to school, education is something that I need to succeed in my life. Instead of horseplaying I'd rather get it done and over with so I can move on to bigger and better things. I need to succeed in life to prove to everyone who has ever done me wrong, that I am independent and just fine without them. —Alycia

When she produced the paragraph above, Alycia was in sophomore English, and she often distracted the class with what we thought was a teenage sense of drama or ill-timed humor. Alycia and her best friend Xena were determined to get and maintain our attention every moment we were in their presence. Their quirky senses of humor tested our abilities to keep a straight face while teaching, but somehow, some way, we managed to guide these two characters toward a focus on what we believed was the good work of our class. Still they remained classic underachievers who almost seemed to be daring us daily to reach and teach them.

While both of these young ladies stumbled through tenth-grade English, they often managed to find their way up to Jim's classroom during the second half of the school's lunch hour when they were supposed to be in the E-room, a large ballroom that was used as something of a transitional space for students during the twenty minutes between lunch and the next class period. While we initially might not have appreciated these young ladies' almost perpetual side conversations and efforts to entertain our class, through these almost daily lunchtime interactions we came to know and appreciate these individuals and their conversations. Eventually they allowed us to participate in their frequently silly, rambling, seemingly pointless exchanges.

Occasionally these conversations would turn to serious topics with which we all had personal experience—difficult relationships with one or both of our parents, family members' battles with alcohol, or their peers' propensities to find increasingly serious trouble. When we announced that we were looking for students to participate in a summer writing and photography project, Alycia and Xena were the first two to post their names. For reasons that we do not recall, Xena ultimately could not partake, but Alycia could—and oh, *did* she.

Alycia engaged with a fervent attention that only a handful of students display. It turned out that behind so many of these preoccupied and disruptive behaviors was a young woman who had experienced a great deal of pain at the hands of the men in her life. And she stunned us—we are in awe still, years later—with her eye for photography. Her images were nothing short of striking, for their composition, light, shape, and tone.

And the writing that accompanied these images was qualitatively different and better than anything we had seen her produce in Jim's class. It was connected, deep, and full of an in-your-face power. She shared more of herself with us that summer over several Saturday mornings than we had learned during her lunchtime visits or in class the entire previous year. We also discovered Alycia's almost profound awareness of who she wanted to be, both in and out of school. Her consciousness of who she was, where she came from, who she thought the world expected her to be, who she longed to become, and her revelations about what seemed like almost ubiquitous moments of courage were remarkable.

This is one of the most significant powers of this project and the TSE strategies: these writing instruction and photo-elicitation methods allow students to *know* themselves as they are and to *learn* about the selves they want to be. The project offers them unique access to their identities, as writers and students and young people. More importantly, it allows them not just to *document*—with images and writings—who they are; it enables them to *create* the selves they ache to enact.

In this chapter, we share four more foundational principles and practices of the Through Students' Eyes method. We also highlight the first of several themes that have emerged in TSE participants' images and writings over the years: how this project allows them to picture their pasts, presents, and futures. We link these notions and illustrations of "self" to three related writing instruction ideas and activities—the concept of Forgetting Our Writer Identities, the practice of Writing by *Not* Writing, and the Arc of Three Writing Conferences.

Picturing Past Selves: Forgetting Writer Identities

FIGURE 5.2

"Somewhere Else"

These are some of my friends. I wanted to see how this picture was going to look, back in the woods. I told them to take off their shirts, so that we could make it seem like we were somewhere else, in another country. Even my father told me that they look like they are in Africa. I like that it looks like it is somewhere else because it's got my brother, friends, and beautiful trees. I would like to go to Africa, because I've never been there. I like this picture because it's all of them together, getting around, taking a picture, showing their muscles. —Demarcus

Demarcus was actually *not* a student in our high school English classes when we met him. He was just eleven years old, and he lived in a public housing development across the street from the community arts space where we conducted our first version of Through Students' Eyes. He would appear at the gallery door every Saturday morning when we were working with Jim's students. He was clearly anxious for a little adult attention, wanting something of a momentary new adventure, hungry for the bit of the breakfast we supplied, and, it turned out, ready to take some gorgeous and compelling images.

We were reluctant to exhibit Demarcus's "Somewhere Else" photograph when we first discovered it and discussed it with him. We were two middle-aged White men, artsy do-gooder teachers, living and working in a neighborhood that was virtually 100 percent African American. We were aware of the complicated positions we occupied. But to display a picture of several shirtless young Black boys, caught looking and acting like they were African children in the bush—this seemed to be too much, too much of a touristy "othering," and likely something that an audience that looked much *more* like the subjects of the picture and much *less* like us might find problematic.

We conferenced with Demarcus at length about his picture, in just the same way that we did with all of our project participants. And it turned out that we could not avoid this image—it jumped out at us, at everyone else who saw it, young and old, and, most importantly, at Demarcus. In the course of our conversations with him, Demarcus shared that, in no uncertain terms, the image made him think of his family's heritage, the history of his race, his personal past. The image represented identity.

Demarcus did not speak in the most complex terms—he was eleven, after all—but he was insightful nonetheless. That is another of the powers of the Through Students' Eyes method: it gives students "ways in" to thinking and writing about their histories, to access ideas and information that might not appear via any other method. They become aware of, gain distance from, and better understand the events in their lives up until now, as pleasant or troubling or innocuous as these events might be.

While these exercises in self-expression and developing students' consciousness of their histories were an important outcome and perhaps one that our students had never before encountered or appreciated, this is not the primary reason that we highlight Demarcus's image and reflection here. As writing teachers, what was most important about our work with him was not his act of remembering, nor was it his or our own or anyone else's consideration of his family's background.

Rather, perhaps the most valuable element of the photovoice work for Demarcus was how this project helped him, and so many of our students, to *forget* identities as writers and students. In forgetting, teachers and students became more open to *learning*, about themselves, their writing abilities and interests, and about our writing pedagogies.

A typical TSE exchange begins like this: a young person and a teacher or other caring adult sit together and look at the students' images on a computer screen or printed and laying on a desk before them. In a typical classroom, teachers would have at least baseline information about students' achievements and experiences as writers. However, the teacher would almost certainly be unaware of the complicated, most often negative beliefs the students had about themselves as writers, based on past experiences and internalized messages.

Via the TSE writing methods and interactions—one young person, one teacher, and one youth's images—the focus shifts away from these conscious or unconscious, nascent or firmly established writer identities, both those students have of themselves and those teachers have formed of them. In these exchanges, teachers begin by simply asking young adults about each of their images, taking more time than a writing instructor or the students typically might to inquire about and discuss the nature, context, and content of each photograph, asking about the young photographer's impressions of each picture, what they liked or did not, what they were thinking when they shot it, and other reflective, insight-oriented questions.

In these interactions, teachers must be diligent about expressing what either *is* or at least *seems* to young people is a sincere interest in each image. We are not suggesting that we feign such curiosity, but that our expressions of interest have to exceed what youth typically encounter in teachers or feel themselves when their writing is being discussed. Such amplified examples of enthusiasm are necessary to help disengaged writers grow in their senses of writing efficacy. We take detailed notes and typically type them for our project participants so that they might consider them in a next round of writing and revision.

Young people are consistently validated and almost universally shocked by the sight of their ideas being honored in such a simple manner. It is obvious that our too often disenfranchised students love and hunger for this level of attention. In fact, these interactions are some of the most profound writing-identity *forgetting* and writing-identity *formation* efforts in which any teachers can engage. It is in these conversations, when we set aside the task of writing and instead concentrate on honoring youths' photographs and highlighting their thinking, that students begin to forget negative experiences with writing and writing instruction.

The act of forgetting results from the fact that we, as teachers, have this other focus—not adolescents' acts of composition, not the words on a page, not their hesitant, on-the-spot oral composing. Rather, we are concentrating on something they have previously believed had little to do with writing: their images on a screen or on the desk. The students are able to release these identities because the writing focus is on something outside of them, rather than on the thoughts inside their heads that they are supposed to articulate.

But it is not just youths' impressions and deep-seated beliefs about their writing identities that must be released if we are to help adolescents to grow into engaged and capable writers. It may be even more important that teachers grow past these established but rarely articulated impressions about youths' writing abilities. Even the best, most sensitive teachers fall into the trap of making assumptions about their students. It may be especially easy to form these impressions with something so foundational to school and life as writing.

The apparently rote act of sitting with a student and honoring their ideas and concentrating on writing by not having these young people write results is both a shock to teachers' unwitting impressions and an almost rhythmic interruption to these inklings. Of course, teachers likely are not conscious of these shocks and rhythms while they are engaged in these interactions with youth. But we have been stunned over and over again by the newfound respect we have for students after we work with them in these structures. And both we and the more than eight hundred young people with whom we have implemented TSE have consistently been impressed by the level of detail and the depth of thought that they share when they are given these different, image-focused opportunities to share.

We begin lessons with these visual tools, which students do not perceive as "school" texts. We concentrate on their photographs—these creative, inescapably personal artifacts that do not immediately appear to be linked to their writing lives. As a result, both young people and teachers are able to forget and see past their negative perceptions about youths' writing identities and the all-too-common characterization of diverse adolescents as "struggling" readers, writers, and students (Streng et al. 2004).

Picturing Present Selves: Writing by "Not" Writing

"The Immigrant's Future"

This taxi car reminds me of why I come to school. I go to school to learn and to have an education in the future and also so I don't end up like those new immigrants who came to the United States and drive taxis. My parents immigrated to America so that we would have a good education and get a good job. I don't want to be a taxi driver like those immigrants because I don't think taxi drivers make really good money and it doesn't give you an education or anything. I also want to make my parents proud of me. Taxi drivers chose that job because they don't have an education and I don't want to be like them. The main reason I come to school is to get an education and have a bright and successful future. —Samar

Samar was one of the now hundreds of youth who participated in our project but who were not actually our students. We have been welcomed into dozens of teachers' classrooms over the past decade to conduct the Through Students' Eyes project and attempt to interrupt diverse youths' too often fragile or negative relationships to writing and school and to help them see new, more positive connections. The writing above that Samar drafted to accompany an image of a large sedan converted to a cab was easily the richest she completed the summer following her eighth-grade year.

Samar was a recent immigrant from Central America, in an eighth-grade class for English-language learners who had developed some rudimentary proficiency with a new language but were not ready to be mainstreamed into classes with their English-speaking middle-school peers. A mature and responsible thirteen-year-old with good study habits, Samar remained almost mute when it came time to speak in English in front of her peers or her teachers. She chatted with her peers like most other young adults, in her native Spanish.

Samar seemed an obvious candidate for TSE. She remained a stereotypical mystery for her teacher, who was eager to try anything to see if she might help Samar develop greater facility and efficacy with English before she started high school. Samar was like so many adolescents who struggle with writing;

she was not disruptive in class and was diligent about trying to mask her writing struggles by presenting as a "good" student. Without such a disruption to Samar's language blocks, these might be her last few months of formal education. She needed an intervention to access her "present" and even begin to help her consider a different "future."

The photovoice composition process involves discussing images in detail, exploring youths' ideas via friendly yet academic conversations, and keeping notes that they will recognize as their own and that they will appreciate as scaffolding for more formal compositions. All of these are key *not-writing* steps in the writing process, and we are sure there are many others that are ultimately useful in our composition procedures. We now rarely ask our students to draft, either by hand or on the computer, the notes that they eventually use to craft reflections about the photographs they have taken. *Not* writing actually appears to be a better bridge into their thoughtful, honest revelations and, ultimately, the development of their abilities to write about relevant topics.

Samar's initial engagement did not come easily, but it was from her that we became aware of that "learning to write by *not* writing" approach. For our students, beginning to write does not have to (and perhaps shouldn't) involve asking our students to engage in the physical act of writing. We might best help students begin to write by *not* writing.

This leads us to one of the most profound insights of our project and the writing instruction methods we have developed: even the investment of a brief one-to-one interaction with a student in the form of an elicitation conference can earn hours and even days of interest and engagement from a youth later on, even the next year should we encounter them in our school or classrooms again. Of course, this teaching/learning equation is not this tidy, but it does seem to be absolute: offer your students even a few moments of these sincere inquiries in one-to-one encounters today and you might just have changed these young adults' entire relationships to you, to writing, and to school.

Like a financial transaction, we "invest" a brief bit of time now and we "earn interest" (i.e., students' engagement in writing activities and school) later. The "dividend" is the profound receptivity that hungry students demonstrate, and the back-end way that their writing improves when we place the focus on *not writing*.

Picturing Future Selves: The Three-Conference Arc

"Not Really Sure What's Right and Wrong"

My little brother Nathan is not doing well in school. He's always in trouble. He was about a "C" student, and then in 7th or 8th grade he started hanging out with the wrong crowd. He started doing some drugs and fighting. I tell him about my uncle who just got out of prison after five years. He's turned his life around: he's now living with his mother, working at Max and Erma's, trying to save for an apartment. He had a daughter and that made him change how he thought about things. He and his wife just got a divorce, so he only sees his daughter on weekends. I don't want my brother to end up like that, having to go to prison. His friends are getting in the way; they are really bad influences. He has other friends who are better to him and who treat him better. They're not really sure what's right and wrong. —Branden

One of the beautiful and sometimes painful elements of this project is the extent to which it has helped us and our students become aware of the realities of their lives. The agonizing aspect of this consciousness is that these youth are often nearly powerless to change the things they see. For example, as his writing above and accompanying portrait of his younger brother reveals, Branden was witnessing his young sibling's apparent academic demise. We know this will sound dramatic, but it wasn't: for whatever constellation of reasons, Branden had made choices throughout his short seventeen years that led him down a path where school mattered, where he had found success in academic pursuits, and he had grown to appreciate them even more, to the point where this now seemed a given, the only path he *could* follow.

He was a working-class Caucasian young man in a community whose demographics were changing quickly. He was stoic but not a shrinking violet. He was confident in his perspective but also inquisitive about new ideas. His peers respected him, though few of them looked like him, and he was admired as a solid member of the Rhodes baseball team. While it might sound like we knew Branden well, we never felt that way. It was only when we invited him to participate in this project and when he began to bring back images that were accompanied by sad, poignant commentaries on his family that we came to understand even a little about what made him tick.

While we never would have anticipated profound insights from Branden, his handful of photographs and reflections offered some of the most telling stories of his life in a crumbling Cleveland neighborhood and school and of the future he saw for himself and his family. He was aware of that thin line between success and frustration in school, between having many choices or no choices beyond high school.

Branden was not able to take credit for his school and athletic achievements to that point in his life; he probably would not have been able to answer what led him to appreciate school and want to be successful in it. Nonetheless, he had grown quite secure in his awareness that he was on the right path, that his was the worldly and more academically and economically promising and higher road. His parents approved and seemed grateful that he was a "good" boy, and college, in some form, seemed a given. But then there was his brother, Nathan.

Nathan was a ninth-grader when Branden was a junior, the year he worked on our project. The two were clearly brothers, with one of the few physical differences between them—besides the height that comes with age—being Nathan's flagrant disregard for anything "good" or "right" with regard to "doing" school. He was not just rejecting school; he was gifted and strident about his denunciation of everything to do with school. He, like almost everyone else, respected Branden, but not enough to temper his contempt for so much of what Branden stood for.

Branden knew his little brother was making small, daily steps toward a life that would ultimately make him very unhappy. Nathan's future would likely be absent a high school diploma, but would probably involve at least petty crime and might eventually include violence, incarceration, or an early demise. Branden did not predict this; he just recognized that Nathan was making the everyday moves in his neighborhood that rarely resulted in anything but such ends.

The Through Students' Eyes project offers something of a parallel to the small steps that Nathan was taking and that Branden was observing and trying to urge his brother to resist. Nathan made increasingly dangerous daily choices to hang out with the "wrong" crowd of his peers. These daily steps would most likely add up to consequences. Similarly, the TSE writing processes must involve small steps, daily choices, and seemingly token activities that take teachers and students down a better, more engaged, more successful writing instruction path.

Students whose writing "pasts" have resulted in negative identities as writers face a common challenge. They have many ideas and the capacity to write, but they need one-on-one attention to help them access the ideas and information they want to share. These one-on-one structures drive our writing instruction. Students are most successful and engaged as writers when we are able to take at least three small steps with them and conduct at least three types of conferences with each youth.

The idea generation conference has already been described in this chapter. In this initial conference, youth consider all of the photographs they have most recently taken, not just the images that most literally answer the project questions or the photographs that students think most obviously address any of these questions. This first conference builds the trust that will allow them to share their most candid ideas and invest most deeply in their writing.

We then provide students with printed copies of the photographs discussed and notes we kept on these first conferences. Based on these first interactions, adolescents draft paragraph-length reflections on two or three different images focused on one of the project questions. In these exchanges, we urge them to consider at least one image that they thought described a less literal response to the questions. Our notes on the first conferences always include some references to these questions, as we return to these in the first one-on-one conference conversations.

The second conference concentrates on these draft paragraphs, with printed copies of their paragraphs and the accompanying images provided. This time we ask youth to read aloud their writings while we read along silently, ready to provide support if they struggle to interpret their writing. The goals of the second conferences, in addition to the standing objective of engaging in affirming interactions, focus on the further elaboration of students' ideas and some attention to word choice.

In these second conferences, we keep and share notes on one or two of the original image/reflection pairs, and we also share the *questions* we have posed to guide these focused elicitations. These questions become the writing equivalent of a reading "think aloud" process: students benefit from the transparency of these processes. They are better able to transfer this writing development procedure to future pieces of writing when they can actually hear, see, and later read the types of questions they might ask to develop their writing.

For the final conference, we consider the revisions students have made to one piece of writing and its accompanying image. By this time these young people have developed a comfort with, even a palpable appreciation for, these interactions. They welcome this attention and the chance to share their ideas. In these conferences, we focus even more closely on word choice and on writing conventions, while making sure that the connection between their writing, the image, and one of the project questions is explicit. We concentrate on the opening and concluding sentences of their paragraphs and making links between these descriptions of the images and those questions of the purposes of, supports for, and impediments to school.

Conclusions

These three (or more) conferences will likely not result in any sort of academic or writing development miracle. The conferences are about kindly and creatively challenging, not once, not twice, but at least three times the decisions a young person might make about her or his engagement with the project, about her or his writing identity, about her or his future.

While it would likely be beneficial to engage with young people in many more and other types of one-to-one interactions around their writing, we typically only have time to conduct three rounds of conferences before we ask students to complete a "final" writing. For youths who are struggling as writers and students, this is about as much attention as they can handle on one writing product. This brief series of one-on-one meetings provides a sufficient foundation for their improved writer and student identities and enhanced writing abilities, as well as for more positive teacher/student or adult/adolescent relationships.

While we appreciate that most classroom teachers might struggle to find the time and structure in a school day to engage with their students in a single writing conference, let alone three over some period of time, we are reminded of the mantra we share with the future teachers with whom we also work.

Preservice teachers frequently ask us if the activities we are sharing with them are "realistic"—are ones they will see in the high school classrooms in which they will eventually observe, in which they will eventually serve.

We candidly and even righteously share with them that they should not expect to see these methods in the *average* English classroom or writing instruction context. Rather, it is our job and their job—as potentially *exceptional* writing teachers—to identify and implement strategies that we know we *should*. Our jobs as teachers and as teacher educators, and perhaps most importantly as *writing* teachers and teacher educators, is to practice and share what is *possible*, not what *is*, with the youth we meet, with the youth whose futures we are given the privilege to consider, via the possibilities they can envision through inquiry-based, visually driven writing instruction approaches.

Picturing Teachers and School

FIGURE 6.1

"Teachers Who Trust You"

This is John Sebabe. He breaks with friends of mine, as much as a couple of times a week in the summer. I go hang out with them sometimes. My friend Tony "Fresh" Velez, who goes to Lincoln-West and is a member of the Cleveland City Breakers, dances with them. He's very good and he's very into it. He is also in drama club at Lincoln-West. The drama teacher lets him do his breakdancing and plan all the dancing in the school plays, even in the Christmas Carol play. Some teachers may not trust you enough to do that. That's what keeps guys like him in school. —Xidi

Xidi, a junior in high school when he took this picture, was one of the first students involved with TSE. He was not only an inconsistent participant in the project, but he was also an increasingly reluctant school attendee. We knew him as a highly intelligent Asian American young man who worked more than fifty hours per week at his family's restaurant and who clearly had already developed a penchant for gambling. While it seemed that everything about his classes and potential future educational opportunities were becoming less important for him as he moved closer to graduation, Xidi was still poignantly aware of what helped his peers to find success in school: their relationships with their teachers.

When we initially asked Xidi about what he thought of school, his reactions echoed those of most of our students and, we would guess, those of the majority of the increasingly diverse and too often disenfranchised high school youth around the United States. He articulately and even angrily complained about what he perceived as the irrelevance of the textbooks and assignments teachers required. He was also highly attuned to the environment and even the aesthetics of the school and his classrooms, expressing a distaste for the perpetually outdated and too often crumbling quality of the buildings and the general dinginess of the classrooms where we interacted with him and his peers.

Given the nature of our project's questions—asking young people to describe and depict their perspectives on school and what helps and hinders their success in it—it is not remarkable that much of what they shared related explicitly to their perceptions of teachers. But the range of what the students revealed was striking, including insights about the relationships they believe teachers should have with students, how teachers should interact with young people, the nature of the curriculum their teachers should be using, and their grander perspectives on school.

In this chapter, we use youths' images and writings to explore some of the traits and habits they would like to find in their teachers and some of the qualities and structures they would like to find in their schools. Several young adults' stories are highlighted to detail insights about the pedagogical principles and teaching practices drawn from years of engaging with youth via these unique, photo-driven writing processes. These include the idea that youths' relationships with teachers are synonymous with their relationships to school; the theory that writing teachers must engage beyond the classroom in order to build relationships in it; the fact that familiarity with students' cultures is not equivalent to having high academic and writing expectations of young people; and the practice of coming in "sideways" with elicitation questions.

Synonymous Relationships: Teachers, School, Writing

"School as Prison"

The clock on the wall ticks down the sentence of the class. It's a constant reminder that schools can act as prisons when teachers don't teach, when students are forbidden to collaborate on what they are "taught." . . . [T]o be completely restricted from speaking during a class defeats the purpose of school. In school you should be taught and able to collaborate on the things you are told by the teacher. Getting an education means that you get some time to learn what your peers comprehend and to compare notes. —Jon

Jon was a whip-smart freshman in the first iteration of TSE at Lincoln-West High School, and as a young White male, he was also in the minority. Jon was comfortable socializing with the diverse group of peers that attended his United Nations of high schools, and he understood that education—and each relationship that was formed through one's involvement in the schooling equation—did not occur in a vacuum. His assumptions about school were seemingly as mature as the institution of school itself; at the least, they seemed to come from an "old soul" source that was revealed as we engaged with him through this project and its methods. His writing above, which was accompanied by a photograph of a school clock, was representative of so many of his reflections and images.

One of the primary lessons of Jon's images and writing related to the criticism of many teachers' practices and schools' structures. Jon's images and words highlighted how the economic and technological boundaries of the so-called real world have morphed and shifted while so much of what we call "education" remains stuck in a much earlier time.

Jon represented the students who are demanding that school become a more relevant institution, on a daily and class-by-class basis, that it more closely reflect the realities of the "real world." Some teachers understand this shift and attempt to make the most of what limited resources disadvantaged urban and rural classrooms might provide, leveraging any possibility to help their students make a connection with school, careers, colleges, and futures. Other teachers see a need to go "back to the basics," a solution a certain percentage of every shade of public school critic suggests as the solution to all of our society's ills.

Jon's photo of the ticking clock and his writing about school as a site of physical, mental, and social constraint had clear and immediate implications for our general teaching and our specific writing instruction practices. His image and reflection forced us to consider more fully those quiet moments in our classes when, while students did not appear to be actively disruptive, their engagement with our content was certainly questionable. Jon challenged us to meet his peers where they were, and he not so subtly implied that we—his teachers—had to do more to make our content germane to his life. Perhaps most importantly, he echoed Xidi's insight that we had to care more deeply about him and all of our students, far beyond any traditional student/teacher relationship and certainly outside of paying attention to their abilities to pass our classes or standardized state tests.

As Jon continued with the photo elicitation activities, it became clear that he was hungry for a closer connection with many of his teachers, particularly those who he deemed worthy of an appropriate adult friendship. We learned that many of his ideas about school and the best, most meaningful, and most effective student/teacher associations had been born of his close relationship to his dad. While his father had not been able to pursue a college degree, he still valued education highly and often spoke with his son about it. The result was Jon's wisdom, his own deep respect for learning, and his critical perspective on his teachers and our school institution.

If this young man taught us one thing about the givens of our students' frequently unstated and most likely unwitting beliefs about school, it was this: youths' relationships with school—and, by extension, their relationships with writing—are virtually synonymous with their relationships with their teachers. It's a simple equation: if we, the teachers, work to enact deeper connections with them, they will be more likely to develop more profound appreciations for the curriculum of our classes, including with what we know is one of the most foundational and most powerful elements of our curriculum—our writing instruction. As well, our students recognize even our attempts to relate to their peers in these more significant ways, though they are generally incapable of and certainly rarely called on to articulate this relationship reality. The tragedy of these relationship equations—involving teachers, youth, and school—is that young people may often subconsciously but very explicitly rebel against school and writing assignments if teachers do not work to develop these deeper student/teacher ties.

We know now that we must become the teachers Xidi describes—ones who use a relationship-oriented approach and trust youths enough that they might engage with school and our literacy tasks in ways beyond what young adults and society in general have come to expect. As White, generally privileged, middle-aged males, we appreciate now that we will never be able to understand what it means to live the lives of our English-language learning students, our African American students, our Hispanic American students, our female students.

But if teachers provide students with opportunities for trust, as Xidi suggests, they just might tell us about their lives and offer clues about where our school and writing goals and their own daily and life needs and objectives might intersect. And maybe, if we show them our willingness to make these connections, they will listen to us about school—or, even better, tell us how school and our writing pedagogies might best serve them.

Engaging Beyond the Classroom to Build Relationships within It

"It's About Passion"

Team sports, in many ways, help you succeed and to accomplish your goals. If I didn't have softball, there would be something missing. Every day before I go to school, even out of season, I am thinking about softball. I am thinking about

FIGURE 6.2

plays, about Ms. Zak, my coach, and about how to help another player when they are having a bad day. Softball is such a big part of my life and if I didn't have it, every day would be gray. Some of my teammates might even drop out of school without it. Softball is about passion; it gives you drive and the desire to succeed. You rely on one another for support. If you don't have those things in school, then you will not succeed. —Samantha

"Goofy"

This picture of Mr. Harmon represents the support I get from teachers like him. Teachers like Mr. Harmon help students like me succeed in school and in life. He is the reason that I like to come to school every day. Mr. Harmon is such a goofy person. He makes learning fun. I know that students love fun learning. He is goofier when he is around Dr. Zenkov. They both remind me of brothers. They always try to comfort other people and take the time to help individuals one at a time. A lot of students enjoy talking to them both. In my opinion they are more than just teachers they are like close friends. Mr. Harmon is a lot of encouragement to a lot of people. Most of his work is interesting and fun but sometimes having too much fun can cause a disturbance when it's time to work. I sometimes can get caught up in excitement stuff and don't want to do anything that involves work. —Chiquitta

We introduced you to Sam in chapter 1, with her positive perspective on her peers and her image "There Are Possibilities." The picture described above (Jim in khaki shorts walking down an uncrowded school hallway), was taken by Chiquitta, who was an introverted and almost unreachable sophomore in Jim's English classroom in Euclid who we worked with several years after we'd met Sam in her Cleveland high school. Chiquitta was the kind of student we went out of our way to reach on a daily basis, even if it meant making fools of ourselves, because we believed that if our antics at least got the attention of a student like her, then maybe she eventually would find our class, the literature we were sharing, and our writing assignments more engaging—or at least more tolerable.

When called on to participate in class—we had a "no tourists" rule—Chiquitta would shrink into herself and avoid eye contact. She would consistently manage to squeak out an answer, but often she had to repeat herself a few times until we and her peers heard her. We were patient and kind with her, never wanting to make her feel self-conscious about her reticent manner. We eventually asked Chiquitta to join the TSE project because we knew it would give her a chance to find the voice she seemed so reluctant to share in our class.

Of course, we did have fun in our classroom, and the students looked forward to Kristien's participation during his regular visits. While it was satisfying to see Chiquitta and her peers respond favorably to our attempts to make English enjoyable—to interrupt the drab rhythm to which they had become so accustomed—Chiquitta's reflection also provided a perspective that we might not have ever considered: there were times when our "goofiness" got things off track for our students and may have even interfered with our instructional goals. According to Chiquitta, there was a fine line—or perhaps an amorphous divide—between what helps one succeed in school and what distracts from youths' focus and achievement. In either event, it forced us to check our assumptions about our practices and our students.

Both Sam and Chiquitta explicitly attempted to address the question of "What helps you to be successful in school?" with their quotes above and the accompanying images—Sam with a picture of her softball team, which was coached by her English teacher, and Chiquitta with an image of Jim, at school on a Saturday with our project. Sam and Chiquitta added an important "how" to the insight that teachers' relationships with students were virtually synonymous with youths' relationships to writing instruction and school.

While many administrators and other so-called experts might caution teachers against being involved in their students' lives outside of the classroom, we know now that we must engage with youth beyond school in order to build those relationships in it, particularly those connections that support effective writing pedagogies. This "beyond" may be interpreted in one of several ways—*beyond* the classroom walls, *beyond* our original perceptions of our students, *beyond* the regular school day, *beyond* our traditionally more distant relationship with our students, *beyond* students' own expectations for school. If a teacher's goal is to improve instruction, all of these "beyonds" must be considered.

Sam and Chiquitta powerfully illustrate how foundational are the roles of teachers' relationships with students in supporting diverse adolescents' writing success. These young adults value teachers who interact with them as people and who care about them as more than one of the dozens of students teachers meet in a day. They do not want us to be their friends but rather to respect them as human beings and to engage with them in richer ways than our standard curricula allows.

While every educator may not need to interact with their students in the way that Sam's coach and we did, every teacher needs to appreciate the relationships they develop with adolescents and the peer networks that result from these teacher-facilitated extracurriculars as supports for students' writing engagement. These young adults' reflections also exhibit that although many of our students' socially oriented pursuits may occur only during a few months each year, young people *continuously* rely on the networks these activities enable. Teachers who develop deeper relationships with students and who engage with them even during one sports season or extracurricular activity might call on these connections to support young adults' engagement with writing tasks for many future class periods, weeks, months, and even years to come.

More controversially, the TSE students expressed that these relationships should be complex, fluid, and rooted in teachers' willingness to cross school and community boundaries. Given that language arts class content often incorporates students' personal writings and responses to literature, as English teachers we appear to be well positioned for developing such relationships and engaging in such boundary spanning. In dozens of images and writings from other youths, we encountered examples of the potentially positive effects of these more complicated, shifting relationships. Many of these pictures and reflections revealed that not only must our notions of our roles as teachers be expanded if we are to best promote our students' writing engagement and achievement, but our very concepts of school must become broader. As well, our analyses of youths' visual and written work suggest that it was the personal nature of these photo elicitation inquiries that allowed adolescents to share insights into the qualities of their associations with teachers who are at once tenacious and forgiving.

Cultural Familiarity Is Not Equivalent to Having High Academic Expectations

"He's Too Nice"

This is a picture of my homeroom teacher. He looks dorky and everything but he's so nice. My homeroom takes a lot of advantage of him. When it's homeroom everyone comes in talking, yelling, [and] screaming. Everyone comes and talks on the phone, and come and go when they please. He never tells them anything. I don't think he ever will. He's too nice. —Maria

Maria was a participant in our first iteration of TSE at Lincoln-West High School, and along with her best friend Sam (whose story and work are highlighted above and in chapter 1), she was one of the more prolific photographers and writers to participate in the ten-plus years we have run the project. We started TSE in 2004 when digital cameras were expensive and clunky, so we resorted to point-and-shoot 35 mm cameras instead. As part of the TSE process, we encourage students to take their cameras with them everywhere and—while remaining conscious of good manners and their own safety—take lots of photographs. Maria was happy to oblige; she shot more than forty rolls of film, or nearly 1,500 images, during the course of the project.

Of course, because TSE asks students to consider the very meaning of school, photographs of school activities and even teachers resulted. Maria did not disappoint: she offered images and intelligent, reflective descriptions. A young woman of Puerto Rican descent, she put greater effort into her school-work in part because, like Sam, she was heavily invested in softball and they wanted to remain as far as possible from that grade eligibility line for participating in extracurriculars.

What seemed most significant about Maria's choice of this picture of her smiling homeroom teacher, a middle-aged White male, and the message in her writing is that this was a veteran teacher in her school, someone who was actually from the community. But he was an educator who appeared to be making a conscious, daily choice not to have high expectations for the behavior or academic achievement of Maria's homeroom classmates. In fact, it seemed that his familiarity and comfort with this community had transformed into an acceptance of others' low expectations.

While Maria's teacher willingly signed a photo release when he was asked if we could include his image in an exhibition of youths' work, we were not surprised when he later contacted us and threatened to sue for libel, defamation of character, and several other popular forms of personal legal recourse. Of course, he had no grounds for taking any such action, but we recognized that the point of our project and of Maria's photograph was not to embarrass any of our students' teachers—our peers. It was more important to Maria, to us, and we think to our readers, that we recognize that her image and writing both extended and complicated the notions of cultural familiarity and of teacher-student relationships.

We have advocated often in this chapter for teachers—and particularly writing teachers—to build closer and more unconventional relationships with their students. But it is important that we never assume that such relationships are, by definition, positive entities, the ultimate objective of a teacher's role, or evidence that an educator will have constructive and high expectations for students. Our most diverse and disenfranchised students cannot—and should not have to—tolerate teachers who appear capable of building relationships and crafting lessons that are culturally relevant or responsive but enact these relationships and implement these lessons without an unadulterated and explicit focus on what is best for these youth, their well-being, and their futures.

Many of the young adults in our project were forgiving of teachers who were inconsistent in their support of students' engagement and achievement—as these teachers too often assumed the worst about these young people and their reasons for failing to show up for or find success in school. But these young people knew that they deserved better than teachers who were afraid of students or who failed to call on them or their peers to follow the basic rules of school. There is tremendous complexity in the relationships teachers form with youth; we must be cautious not to assume that we know more about students than is accurate or with which they are comfortable. We might exercise even a higher degree of caution if we are from these same communities—because our students may be more likely to accept our more critical assessments of their abilities, which may be low in part because of the familiarity we possess.

Such a conflation of close relationships, cultural familiarity, and low expectations for students is particularly problematic with regard to students' writing engagement and achievement and with our writing instruction, for at least three reasons.

First, writing is arguably the most foundational of all activities in school; writing is an activity in which students engage in every class. Second, while one could contend that writing and reading are equally important across subject areas and to students' future school and life success, we would argue that writing is potentially more necessary to get "right" from an instructional standpoint—because it is a creative, constructive act rather than consumptive endeavor.

Finally, while much of the writing schools call on students to do may not appear to be personal—for example, writing essays, research papers, and more—the act of writing is always a very personal, individual act. It is always inseparable from one's intellectual, individual, and even social identity. This is a reality that very few teachers and even a smaller percentage of the general populace seems to recognize—to the detriment of our diverse students' writing success and engagement.

Coming in "Sideways" with Elicitation Questions

FIGURE 6.3

"My Beliefs"

Christianity is my religion, and I hate subjects in school that challenge my religion. I didn't like the unit on evolution, because it tells me that my religion isn't true. "Facts" leave no room for possibilities. I don't really care if it's true that I came from a primate. We're a lot like monkeys. But when [teachers] challenge how the earth was made this bothers me. The Bible tells us how the Earth was made, but don't tell me what to believe. I see this happening a lot in school. I wouldn't want to participate in a class where my ideas are being insulted and there isn't room for my beliefs. —Jonnatan

We met John in his freshman year. He joined us for the project during his junior year, by which time we had a good sense of who he was as a person and a student. He was extremely thoughtful: he was a part of an honors track that started with about forty students in his ninth-grade year but included fewer than twenty by the time his cohort reached senior year. John not only engaged with us when we implemented Through Students' Eyes in his junior English class, but he dutifully showed up for nearly every after-school and summer gathering when we continued the project beyond the end of the school year.

All of his teachers and most of his classmates would have described John as a friendly, sometimes almost painfully intelligent, and a hyperactive young man. He was not diagnosed as having ADD or ADHD; he was just characteristically high-energy, particularly with his speech patterns. His family was not able to offer him much support with his academic efforts. His mom, like so many of our Cleveland students' parents, had not been able to earn her high school diploma, and she most readily found employment in the health services sector. When we met John, she was working a third-shift job in a residential youth detention center. For reasons we did not understand, John lived an uncompromising ethic of doing what was expected of him: he was respectful in class, energetic at every turn, and didn't hesitate to complete the assignments his teachers offered.

Yet the pictures he took for TSE were often ones that required elaborate explanation in order for any viewer to appreciate why he had selected these as relevant to the project questions. In fact, when we studied John's images with him, often even *he* didn't seem to be able to immediately recall or articulate just why he had taken particular photos. John seemed almost permanently distracted. Every conversation with him was an interesting tangential stream-of-consciousness. We knew that he was serious about exploring and sharing his perspectives via images and writing. And he was earnest in a way that suggested that he was hungry for the attention that we provided, indicating that he knew there was something valuable in these interactions and the project itself, even if he wasn't sure what.

John represented a challenge typical of youth faced with a writing task. These students have many ideas and they have the capacity to write, but they need one-on-one attention to help them access these ideas and the information they want to share.

As we described in the last chapter, at the core of our writing instruction methods are the series of elicitation conferences we implement with youth, sometimes in multiple sessions around a single image. Exhibiting even the tiniest bit of frustration with seemingly unmotivated or distracted youth or with apparently irrelevant or superficial visual and written responses to the project questions is a surefire way to turn a student off. Our task is to inquire again and again, with every bit of sincerity we can marshal, about why a young person took a particular picture.

Asking students questions is a combination of art and science, and the process of using images as a foundation for a reflective and writing practice is both freeing and stifling. The idea of answering questions with pictures is confusing to youth. (It's actually a little mind-bending for most adults, too.) Additionally, young people who are disengaged from school are simultaneously reluctant to share their perspectives and anxious to tell teachers and the world just what is wrong with our schools, educational system, teachers, schedules, and texts.

Sample Elicitation Questions

- What do you like about this image?
- Why did you take this picture?
- What does this photo say about you?
- What are the important details in this photo?
- What would you title this photograph? Why?

The elicitation questions we typically use are listed in appendix 6.1 at the end of this chapter. But these questions are merely the starting point for effective elicitation and writing activities. The real art of these interactions—the points at which we and our students are most engaged and they produce the most honest and compelling reflections—occur when we grow comfortable enough to develop and pose follow-up and alternative questions in the moment, while we are sitting with these youths and their photographs.

Young people who have found little but frustration in school and with writing are initially oriented toward very straightforward, literal, and "right" answers to the project questions. Many of these young adults begin with fairly obvious photographic responses to the project's questions. They are accustomed to mixing media (e.g., images and text) in their out-of-school literacy practices, but they were not as familiar with blending these modes in academic activities. The open-ended elicitation questions, supported by one-on-one and small group discussions and writing conferences, provide youth with the freedom to develop wider and more personal sets of ideas.

The list of questions included almost invariably results in adolescents' thoughtful responses and the foundation for meaningful writing. But when we listen carefully to them, we are able to pose questions that really matter to them. When we come in "sideways" and ask about things other than their perspectives on school, our students often have breakthroughs.

John's image and writing above are a perfect, poignant example of this responsive, "sideways" elicitation process. At first glance, and even after some initial conversation with John about his photograph of The Last Supper painting, we were unsure about its relevance to our project and its questions about school, and we were unclear how our consideration of this image might support John's writing engagement and development. We were persistent with posing many of the queries listed to John, keeping notes on his responses so that he might use these in the next step of our writing process.

But it was only when we heard him articulate a quite nuanced idea—the difference between a "fact" and a "belief"—that we were able to access what really mattered to him about this photograph. Only when we followed this line of questioning, deviating from our standard list of queries, did he express what we eventually came to understand was a very troubling phenomenon. John did not hold creationist beliefs that rejected any notions of scientific evidence. Rather, he was a devout Catholic who longed for his teachers to appreciate that there was a difference between faith and fact. Most importantly, he expressed that it wasn't so much that his biology teacher did not seem capable of holding two such apparently contradictory thoughts in his head at one time. Rather, John was troubled that his teacher was intentionally disregarding such an important element of his own and his community's life—their faith, their religion.

Ultimately, John reminded us of the nature of a teacher's "stance": it is not so much the information we share that matters to our disenfranchised students, to our disengaged writers. Rather, it is how we listen, it is that we pay attention to their perspectives that will help them find a "way in" to our subject matter, to writing, and to school and perhaps to the opportunities that knowing content, growing as writers, and being successful in school will eventually afford.

Appendix 6.1

Elicitation Questions

Opening Questions

- What is the first thought that comes to mind when you look at this photo?
- What do you like about this image?

"Why" Questions

- Why did you take this picture?
- Did you take this picture on purpose or accidentally?
- What does this photo say about you?
- How is this photograph personal to you?

"Where" Questions

- Where did you take this picture?
- Who were you with when you took this picture?

"When" Questions

- What was happening when you took this photo?
- What happened just before or just after you took this photograph—to you or the people in the image?
- What is happening just outside of the frame of this picture?

Feeling Questions

- How does this photograph make you feel?
- What do you think your friends, family, teachers, parents, or others would feel or think about this picture?

Audience/Conclusion Questions

- What do you want others to see/think when they look at this photo?
- If you were to present this picture to our class, what would you want to say?

People in the Picture Questions

- What is the person in this photograph thinking, feeling, and seeing?
- How do the people in this photograph feel about each other?
- What would someone who knows the person in this photograph say about it?

Descriptions

- What do you see in this photograph?
- What are the important details in this photo?

Sentence Starters

- I like this picture because . . .
- I took this picture because . . .
- I think this is a good picture because . . .
- I think this picture will confuse people who see it because . . .

Project Questions

- How does this picture answer the question, "What is the purpose of school?"
- How does this picture answer the question, "What supports your school attendance and achievement?"
- How does this picture answer the question, "What gets in the way of your school attendance and achievement?"
- How does this picture answer the question, "What makes a 'good' teacher?"

Title Questions

- What would you title this photograph? Why?
- Are there words from your writing that would be a good title?

7

Picturing Challenges and Trauma

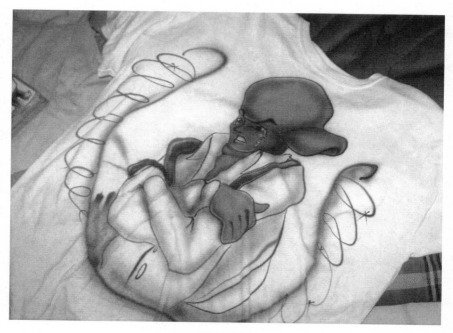

FIGURE 7.1

"Brother in the Sky"

The memory of my brother Deyshaunne sometimes keeps me from being successful in school. It gets in my way because I sometimes daydream thinking about him and how much fun we had together. I would daydream in class about how much I miss him and how we used to joke around and play video games together. It saddened me deeply when he died because we were so close and we did everything together. When he died it sent me into a drought in school because it felt like I lost my best friend. In school I shut down and let my grades fall dramatically. By my brother dying it really got in the way of my success in school. —Daijon

Daijon was a reticent, young, African American man who admittedly kept to himself and did not hesitate to share his skepticism about things in school that he had deemed were a waste of his time. He told us, however, that he liked our classroom because of its "energy" and because he felt few of his teachers asked him to work collaboratively. He was enamored with the idea of "collective genius" that he felt was a big part of the class.

Daijon was thrilled—and suddenly not so taciturn—when we had our gallery showing of his TSE work. In his words, this exhibition "gave me a chance to share my issues in [different] ways [than the ones] I wasn't always comfortable with. Most people gave me a hard time because they thought I was lazy. I know I was [just] quiet."

Years after his graduation from high school, Daijon reflected on TSE. He said he appreciated the chance to process multiple traumas on his own, in writing elicitation conferences, and via the public through his image and writing. "I hated writing. I wrote a bunch of crap in high school. (TSE) showed me I was good at it and there was something productive from it."

It was clear from the writing he crafted during the course of our summer project that family was the centerpiece of Daijon's life. In a reflection accompanying another image he took that summer, he wrote:

> My family is what keeps me motivated to be successful in school. They keep me motivated because they are always on my back about staying active in school and doing all my school and class work. My family has great expectations for me to do amazing things in life.

The pressure on Daijon and other siblings to fill voids in the family life through the tragedy of losing a child was not lost on him. Daijon knew that the stakes had grown much higher, and he owned them with reservation.

Daijon's story points out the sober truth that, after a brief leave, students are expected to come to school and do their best, even after a devastating loss. How can such traumas, large or small, *not* impact relationships to writing and school? Perhaps an even more obvious and important question is: Given these sad distractions, why would students value the writing assignments and strategies we ask them to complete?

Although we do not ask students to write about trauma or tragedy, it is frequently the story a photograph literally or metaphorically tells. This chapter covers a range of writing instruction principles and practices that seem to honor these difficulties and help youth to work through them. They include the idea and practice of Explicitly Explaining the Assumed and Everyday and One-to-One or Not at All. We also describe and illustrate the principles and strategies of Just Ten Minutes—Seriously, Ten Minutes and Apparently the Mundane Matters.

Explicitly Explaining the Assumed and Everyday

"What Is Your Name?"

Some things that make me unsuccessful in school are teachers, assignments, and friends. I have some teachers who always give me a lot of homework. I don't always understand the directions or the assignment, so I fall behind. Sometimes the teachers get mad at me and yell, so I am sad and feel like they don't like me. Some of the assignments I do in school seem boring to me. I don't feel motivated to finish them, so I don't learn as much as I'd like to. Then I fail the test because I didn't learn the way I should have. . . . I moved to the United States in 2006. When I arrived, I only knew how to answer the question, "What is your name?" Since then, I have learned a lot more English, but sometimes I still get confused when I hear long words that I don't know the meaning of or when people talk too fast. So many words sound the same, but are spelled differently, so writing can be hard for me as well. —Archana

Archana, a recent immigrant from Nepal, was practically mute in the language arts class for English-language learners where we met and worked with her with the TSE project. She sat up ramrod straight in class and simulated the behaviors of an engaged student. While she made incomplete efforts to finish her writing assignments, she did not seem to have the English proficiency to achieve in the way she and we hoped, and she appeared inconsistently but occasionally resistant to our assignments.

At least that is what we believed until we began to meet with her in one-to-one writing conferences, and she eventually produced the reflection above that accompanied a picture of her wire-bound notebook and one of her school assignments. Our students tell us that these conferences are foundational to their success with our writing activities. However, as Archana's story demonstrates, even these relationships may not be sufficient to ensure success in English classes.

As an interpersonal connection with Archana in conferences began to build engagement, we recognized that the primary challenge she was facing was one of simply not understanding some of the minutiae of our writing instruction and of school in general.

Archana represents one of the most frequently mentioned and straightforward desires for writing curricula and pedagogies: an absolute clarity in assignment guidelines and explicit naming of the general rules of school operation. Students are often part of an institution that they simply did not understand—after a few months, after years, or, in the case of even youth who are not immigrant or English-language learners, after generations.

Language challenges were certainly an impediment to Archana's interest in and success with writing. However, a greater concern to her was the cultural and institutional variances in which these language differences were embedded. And if a student is struggling to read, interpret, and perhaps articulate confusion about even the apparently straightforward directions on an assignment, then she is even less likely to feel confident about and be able to express herself about the nature of a more global confusion, such as about the basic norms of a classroom or an institution.

Archana's confusion has been echoed in the writings and conversations with the vast majority of our students and project participants. When these young people do not even attempt to complete assignments in classes or finish a daily writing activity, too often the reason is because they are just puzzled by the directions or the task itself. This silent confusion is complicated and amplified by the fact that they are painfully insecure about their abilities to intelligently express their questions, not to mention to complete their writing assignments.

Writing assignments may be some of the most challenging activities that our students encounter, often causing them to question their abilities to function in classrooms and schools. Perhaps this is because writing is inherently a personal affair. Unlike a math equation or a chemistry lab or even a recounting of historical events, nearly everything to do with writing involves a personal orientation. Maybe the deep difficulty with our writing tasks is due to the fact that writing—like reading but arguably to an even greater extent—is foundational to every content, to every class. So an individual might feel less than proficient with writing, and this feeling of inadequacy—or actual writing difficulties—naturally carries over to *all* subject areas. Reading is also a cross-curricular skill, but it is not one that calls on a student to *produce* something or to reveal themselves in the same way that writing requires.

As well, we wonder now how a young person might express a distaste for or a frustration with writing when this skill is so foundational to everything we do in school and particularly in our English classes. Young people cannot rightly say they do not "like" to write: writing is a given, whether it is jotting down our names at the top of a test or drafting a massive research paper in a word processing program. So, instead, our students—and especially our disenfranchised, increasingly diverse, and often immigrant youth—simply, and most often passively, resist. They do not do their work. They do not write their names. Why? Because they need the assumed and the everyday to be explained again, by teachers who they trust and who clearly care enough about them—and not just their assignments—to build relationships with them.

One-to-One or Not At All

"Barriers"

I took the picture of the flag with the barbed wire in front of it because I think it represents the barriers that get in the way of students reaching their goals. Some of the things it represents are drugs, hanging out with the wrong people, bad parenting and babies from having sex. I know a lot of people who have dropped out of school and all of those things have played a role in at least one of my friends as the reason they dropped out. I think if the people know what gets in the way, they will help prevent it from happening. That's why I took the picture. —Tim

Tim drafted the writing above to accompany an image of a US flag waving above a stark sky and a very secure factory facility in his neighborhood. Initially he was very reluctant to discuss this photograph, as he perceived that it did not literally and explicitly address any of our project questions. We recall many uncomfortable moments of interaction with Tim when he participated in the first version of our project. He was a stoic young man of Eastern European descent and rarely said a word in our classes. We wondered: Was his silence evidence of some pain or a disability? Was it proof of his disinterest in all things writing and school? Was it something with which we should be pedagogically concerned, or was it just his personality and something with which he would find a way to work, find a way in the world?

Then we met Tim's mom, Laurie, and much about his motivations and his frustrations—for our project, for school, for so much more—became clear. If Tim was reticent, his mom was a chatterbox. She filled every potential void in every conversation, and not just those in which she was directly involved. We loved her and Tim appreciated her, though it was clear that her energy and ready tongue left little room for him to offer his own ideas.

But what was even more evident was that Tim's mom was very aware of the educational and life opportunities on which she and her family members had missed out, and she was not going to allow Tim to know such dissatisfaction. While Tim might not have appreciated TSE as something in which he was interested, his mom saw our project as a free extracurricular, as something that not many young people in our depressed city and its underresourced schools would typically be afforded.

Laurie was one of the few adults—family members, teachers, and preservice teachers from Kristien's university—who took us up on our invitation to support these young people in our project activities. We believed that their weekly or even occasional presence at our sessions could only help to forge that school/community bridge—that these adult family members' and teachers' understanding of the activities in which the youth of their lives were participating could only be a good thing. And that their knowledge of these young adults' ideas about school could only serve to help them reflect further about how to best serve the adolescents for whom they were responsible.

But Tim's mom and her mode of interaction—well meaning but protective—complicated our assumptions and our procedures, and she eventually led us to an important realization about our writing elicitation structures. The fact was that Tim's mom was an expected partner: Tim participated in our project as much because of his mom as the result of our invitation. Prior to this project, we still approached writing conferences as if they should only focus on students' growth and with the idea that they were as much a management method as an instructional tool. That is, we thought these interactions would allow us to reteach some desperately needed remedial writing skills to individual students who were hopelessly distracted and even disruptive in our classes. But Tim woke us up to the real potential and importance of these exchanges.

One of the key insights we made after these interactions with Tim—almost to defend against the interactions when his mom was involved, attempting to be supportive, but leaving little space for Tim—was about the very nature of these writing conferences. While effective as momentary instructional interludes that allowed us to offer minilessons on one writing topic or another, they served a much grander purpose: they shifted the focus away from the initial impressions Tim and we had of his writing struggles, and away from the ideas that his mom shared, and toward positive writing identities.

Tim reminded us that we needed to be cautious about the assumptions we make about young people and that we must incorporate writing instruction practices that allow us to fill in the blanks of what we do not *yet* know about these youth. And he taught us that with many of our students, if we want them to write and care about writing and if we want them to begin to engage with school in the ways we all hope, we have to meet with them in these intimate settings. For so many of them, real engagement in school—and especially with writing—begins with these one-to-one conferences or not at all. It is often only through these intimate interactions with young people that we can help them to "translate" their established, learned defensive stances toward writing into more open and positive relationships. For example, it is via these one-to-one exchanges that we repeatedly relearn that when a young person states that they "do not like to write" that they are really just reminding us that they have had far more negative than positive experiences with writing instruction in school.

Of course, we have been challenged by when and how to conduct these conferences. Full-time classroom teachers cannot simply pull students aside, into even a semiprivate setting, and spend substantial time or even more than a few minutes with just one young person. We first began to see the results of these conferences when we were able to conduct them with summer participants in our project—when we were not simultaneously responsible for a whole class of teenagers while we were meeting with individuals.

But the tremendous outcomes of these summer interactions convinced us that these one-to-one exchanges were important enough that we simply had to find a way to conduct them in school, if only occasionally, with students in our language arts classes and those involved with the Through Students' Eyes project. A teacher's effective integration of these structures is much more about an ethic, about seeking and taking advantage of as many opportunities for momentary exchanges, than it is about actually having designated periods during the course of an instructional day to engage with young people in these contexts. Such interactions do not need to be lengthy, as the writing instruction we are doing is focused much more on engaging with young people to help particular ideas and practices to "stick" than it is about offering formal minilessons.

Just Ten Minutes

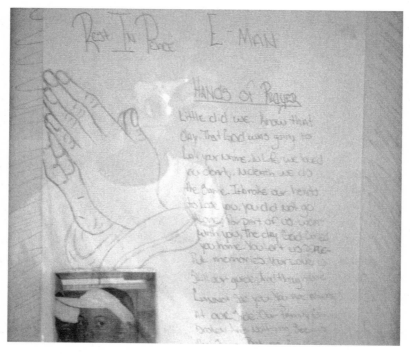

FIGURE 7.2

"Eman"

This is a photograph of my friend Eman and a poem from his obituary. Eman
had a difficult life with many obstacles to overcome. Unfortunately he was not
able to overcome them. I made this image to help motivate me by reminding
me of things that he had to go through that I do not want to go through. It also
helps to remind me of things to look out for. The death of family members,
especially young family members, can get in the way of school. It is hard to
concentrate on school when you are dealing with the death of someone you are
close to. It makes it even more difficult to deal with when things like this keep
happening. —Gordon

Gordon, like many of the students who participated in the TSE program,
had not yet demonstrated a strong sense of his own writing voice. One on
one, Gordon was charming and even disarming, with his deep, dark eyes and
radiant smile—an affect that belied the fact that he spoke in almost a whisper
and was timid.

Although the female students in our class were not shy in the least about
their collective belief that Gordon was a catch, this admiration didn't follow
through to his teachers. Gordon did his work, never acted out, was the last
young student to be asked to "quiet down" by a teacher, and was willing to
partner with any of his peers. Yet he was often dismissed as unremarkable.
We were grateful that he *never* drew our attention for negative reasons, but
we were also concerned that he also rarely required us or his peers to notice
him for positive reasons, either.

In ten minutes during a summertime TSE session, all that changed. Gordon engaged with the idea of writing with a purpose, and his writing opened
up—all in one project session. Gordon took those ten minutes of one-on-one
time and turned them into surprisingly powerful photographic and written
reactions. Ten minutes were enough to build a connection with an attentive
and caring adult, to open to the idea of the project, to formulate ideas, and
to write about them in a more independent way. It was enough to engage his
passion and give him purpose—and a voice.

If we had to argue for a single shift in any teacher's pedagogy, these fleet-
ing conferences would be it. They may be the most valuable ten minutes we
ever spend as teachers. Writers' conferences do not have to be *lengthy* in
order to be beneficial. Gordon was just one of hundreds of the illustrations of

the power of such short, dedicated interactions with a compassionate adult. These ten minutes of time with a caring adult who even *appears* to be interested in a youth's life, photographs, ideas, or writings can have a profoundly positive impact on a teenager's overall confidence, academic efficacy, writing idea development, or willingness to trust teachers and school.

A "how-to" guide to the Ten-Minute Writer's Conference is located at appendix 7.1 at the end of this chapter.

The Apparently Mundane Matters

FIGURE 7.3

"For My Mother to Know"

The reason why I go to school is to make it. It's to know one day I will reach my hand out to receive my diploma and to know that my mother will be so proud of me. For my mother to know that I will succeed in life and for me to know that I'm going places. This picture is not quite clear because I'm not there yet. —Ebony

Ebony was a sophomore English student. She had moments in class where she would unconsciously stare off into space, mouth agape, clearly lost in some thought, and she was often the target of jokes because of this. She never seemed to take the teasing seriously; Ebony had one of those kind hearts that allowed her to be sweetly oblivious to the barbs of her peers.

About halfway through the year we learned that Ebony's mother was very sick and awaiting an organ transplant. As we began a TSE session at the end of that school year, we learned that Ebony's mother had passed away. We assumed that this tragedy would mean the end of her involvement in the project, but Ebony found a way. She missed only one week of our summer work together.

For our students, sometimes the purpose of education is just to complete something they started, and school success comes from just showing up. Ebony's graduation was a gesture of love for her mother. Ebony's image and writing, and her commitment to the project under difficult circumstances, remind us that many of the diverse and disenfranchised young people in our classrooms are anxious—perhaps desperate—for opportunities to make sense of their lives. They are hungry for the even momentary extra attention that projects like TSE provide.

We have shared Ebony's image with many other young people and many other audiences over the years of our project. When we do so, we note that this was not a picture that Ebony initially selected as one worthy of attention or one that offered important lessons. Yet every audience, including and particularly other young people, appreciate this picture greatly and resonate with the sentiments shared. They assume that the blurry quality—evidence of a "bad" picture—was actually an intentional choice by Ebony. And they recognize that what might be a given in so many youths' lives—graduating from high school—is hardly automatic for many in their communities.

There is a vital lesson about writing instruction in this photograph and Ebony's reflection: What we might consider stereotypical, mundane, or even clichéd subjects in our youths' writings and images are actually hugely relevant and motivating topics for students who are struggling with school and writing. That is, these explorations of fairly standard topics do not have to concentrate only on the ordinary, popular details that it seems all of us know about such subjects. Our elicitation conferences and repeated but patiently offered sets of probing questions often provided these youth with "ways in" to nuances about these subjects that neither they nor we had discovered previously. When we allow young adults to engage in a writing process and do not judge the seemingly superficial nature of their writing topics, they begin to see writing as a meaningful activity.

We keep up with many of the former TSE participants via social media, including Ebony. Since her high school graduation, Ebony, now known by her nickname "Mackey," has forged a successful personal and professional adult life, working as both a toddler teacher at a local day care facility and as a much-sought-after hair and career stylist. "I love doing both, but I've decided to pursue a dream of having my own business as a hair and career stylist." According to Ebony, "career styling" involves helping individuals to consider and improve their complete physical appearances, and she takes pride in styling the look of many local hip-hop and R&B acts.

Ebony reflected on her participation in our project several years ago and the impact it had during such a tumultuous time in her life. "It really helped me process my emotions, helped me understand my place in the world. After my mother had passed and I didn't really know how to feel, I decided I had to come back to the project and keep going with it. Taking pictures and writing about the meaning of them helped me realize that I had a creative side, and in a way, helped me become the strong woman I am today."

Appendix 7.1

The Ten-Minute Writer's Conference: A How-To

While the Just Ten Minutes exchanges vary in content and structure, they generally follow several key principles, practices, and steps, deconstructed here.

Teachers should take every opportunity possible to engage other adults in their classes, looking to the following individuals and others for support with ten-minute writing conference interactions:

- local universities' preservice teachers
- that occasional university education professor who still enjoys interacting with youth
- the special education teachers with whom you are teaming
- a wandering administrator in your building
- a willing colleague with a planning period, perhaps someone for whom you will return the favor
- trusted family members of your students (with accompanying background check)

If the adults who are willing to support these conferences are reluctant to actually engage in these intense interactions, teachers might ask them to "cover" the entire class while you work with youth in a corner of your classroom or in the hallway. Yet with some rudimentary instructions, any adult can work with even the most reluctant writer in these settings by:

- being positive about a young person's potential interest in writing and/or her/his ability to be successful with writing
- simply devoting that gift of ten minutes of time and dedicated attention to a young person's writing efforts
- approaching young people with an awareness that they may not appear to appreciate these interactions, but remaining quietly confident that youths value adults' willingness to invest in them and their efforts to build even brief but real relationships with them

It is vital that teachers who are looking to other adults and professionals as supports for conducting such conferences offer students some key structures and ground rules for these periods when the rest of the class will be expected to operate independently:

- sell and preach the value of these interactions to your students from the first day of instruction
- scaffold students into these exchanges, beginning with three-, five-, and seven-minute versions during the first several weeks of the school year
- provide students with meaningful independent work, with which they will be more likely to engage without interruption while you are conducting writing conferences
- preach "The FOG" (the Fear of God—the clear identification of reasonable consequences from you) to ensure that the rest of your students in a given class or larger group setting will engage independently and rather quietly at their own desks
- share the writing results of these interactions with your administrators; doing so will not only provide students with new, different, and more authentic ways to be honored in school but it will also serve as evidence to persuade your school leaders to support you with the implementation of these one-on-one structures.

Students are often palpably uncomfortable with these conferences when teachers begin to conduct them:

- They simply have not interacted with many teachers in this way, except when they have been reprimanded for classroom misbehavior or a failure to perform required academic tasks.
- To counteract this discomfort—which young people will often express as distaste or dismissal—teachers must persistently and repeatedly express genuine interest in the ideas youths express in their writing.
- Remember that the overall rapport and positivity generated throughout your classes across the rest of the year often seem almost miraculous.

We offered a sample list of the elicitation questions we use in these conferences in chapter 6. Ultimately, these questions and these ten-minute exchanges are art and science, rooted in the art of the teacher-student rela-tionship. Youth who *know* their teachers or some other caring adult through these intimate interactions *trust* these same people more in whole class and other school settings. As a result, they are willing to engage with so many more and other activities and complete so many additional and different as-signments that they simply would not have otherwise.

8

Picturing Family and Community

FIGURE 8.1

"My Dad"

I took pictures of my stepfather because he helps me out so much. He supports me with everything that I do; he puts food in my stomach, and a roof over my head. He's a very big part of my life and a great influence. He pushes me so much and tells me I could do better. He motivates me a lot, as does the rest of the family. Overall I took lots of pictures of my family because they support and help me so much. They motivate me a lot. I have a wonderful family. —Neena

Neena was a student who, from her earliest academic life, simply knew how to do school well. She was clearly bright, but what really distinguished her from her peers was her motivation to achieve in her classes and her ability to navigate the educational terrain that confounded so many of her peers. Her upbringing and family experiences did not predict that she would care so much about and be so successful in school. Neena herself, through her reflective, metacognitive photo-elicitation work, impressed upon us the near-shock she still exhibited at her lengthy track record of school success.

Neena's writing demonstrated that the relationship on which she counted most was with the man she called her stepdad, although he was no longer married to her mother and had no legal ties to Neena. Yet she lived with him during high school, and he was unfailingly supportive of her school endeavors, including her writing pursuits and particularly the photography and composition activities in which we engaged her through this project. She and many other students demonstrated the unanticipated role that such nonfamily "family" members, and the larger community, played in youths' lives.

Writing to Redefine "Family"

Neena's image, reflection, and story actually highlight two writing instruction lessons from the photovoice methods. The first is that we should never assume the nature of "family" or who plays supportive, or destructive, roles in our students' lives, particularly with regard to who influences their relationships to writing and their development as writers. The networks of individuals who our diverse young people count as "family"—who influence their writing and school relationships—are comprised of a much more expansive array of individuals than we might expect.

The second insight is even more important. Writing and photo-elicitation methods are particularly useful for helping youths to develop an *awareness* of who these individuals are, the roles they play, the functions young people would like them to perform if they are to be successful with writing and school, and how these roles evolve and change. Through picturing and writing about family (and "family") members, students discover they might be able to develop the abilities to influence this evolution.

In follow-up conversations, Neena described how this project had not only allowed her to reflect on the place of school in her life but also to share her perspectives with her peers, teachers, and family/"family," as well as the audiences of our project's publications, exhibitions, and website. She reminded us that our writing instruction practices and even schools' structures often limit teachers' opportunities to engage with struggling students in the immediate ways that they require. While these young people have very adult experiences and opinions about life and school, typical school structures and traditional teacher/student relationships are not conducive to interactions with youth in the mature ways they need to sufficiently honor their ideas.

This inquiry into the nature of youths' families and how these core networks support and sometimes impede our students' abilities to engage and be successful with writing and school in general leads to important details of our students' lives. For example, via our photo-elicitation methods, Neena and many other TSE students disclosed and processed the reality that the financial challenges their adult family members were facing were actually issues with which these adolescents were concerned daily.

They revealed to us that the writing endeavors should be ones that provide students with opportunities to share the challenges they and their families are encountering and to suggest solutions to these difficulties. These adolescents believed schools should be supporting their families with employment counseling classes and access to training, as well as educating youth in the means to attain some measure of future financial stability. Somewhat paradoxically, the students also wanted schools to respectfully remind adolescents that their primary concern should be with engaging with school rather than worrying about and even actively contributing to the financial solvency of their families.

Writing instruction practices that serve our diverse urban adolescents might, then, appreciate the range of relationships these young adults form, from traditional family and friends to individuals with whom they have no blood connections or with whom they would appear to have few links, and even to role models and mentors in their lives. Writing practices that inquire about the ways in which these individuals beyond peers and family members support their engagement and achievement in school are particularly useful.

The existence and qualities of these relationships cannot be assumed in our most intensified, economically impoverished school and community settings. Rather, these relationships—like our concepts of literacy curricula and teachers' roles—should be *living* questions. Allowing our students to keep asking and answering the question of what are the most relevant relationships to their literacy success may be one of the most promising practices of the TSE work. Again, this inquiry involves authentic, very personal, and quite motivating "ways in" to some of the very literacy skills toward which we are directing our students.

The Importance of "Photo Walking"

"My Life"

This is a picture of a gun. It is black and 57 inches long. This gun represents protection. . . .The gun reminds me of my dream and goal, which is to become an Air Force officer. I want to be an Air Force officer because they don't always go to war or die, but they still help the country. I want to protect the United States because there are a lot of bad people in the world and we need to stop them. For example, I want to help stop illegal immigrants from coming to the United States. The gun is a way for me to protect people and this country. Even though I am originally from Panama and came to the United States three years ago, I still want to serve the United States. In order to reach my goal, I need to become a good reader and writer. Reading and writing are my protection, just like the gun. When I read and write, I gain the knowledge and feel smarter than other people. I am no longer ignorant, but I know more information. The purpose of reading and writing is to protect me, like the gun, against ignorant people and bad thoughts. —De'Andre

De'Andre was not only an especially attentive young man and student, but he was practically a poster child for the complex and even seemingly incongruous demographics we face in diverse urban or ex-urban schools in the United States. He was a recent immigrant to the United States, but he arrived in our northern Virginia community under quite different conditions than what most stereotypes about immigrants suggest. His family was well educated in a formal schooling sense, and he was very much a legal immigrant. A native Panamanian, he was both Black and of Latino origin.

De'Andre was unique in a number of other ways. He was aware of the immigration controversies in the United States, and his professional goal was to help ensure that future "illegal" immigrants would not so easily enter his adopted country. Of course, many of the youth by whom De'Andre was surrounded in his middle school class, his school, and his community were ones who he would not have allowed into the United States. He saw no tension in this fact, but he did appreciate that reading and writing would help him to achieve this xenophobic goal. We did not emphasize this tension in our interactions with De'Andre.

Perhaps because he feared we would challenge his perspective, De'Andre did not readily share this stance, his goals, or his motivation behind learning to read and write in English. In fact, he knew how to "do" school well enough that he initially offered many literal, concrete answers that might have applied to the general population of students, not only his individual experience.

D'Andre's writing broke open and he was able to consider grander, more nuanced, and more honest responses to our elicitation questions as he participated in "photo walks." The photo walk ranks with the elicitation conferences as one of TSE's most powerful tools. It is an exercise that not only enables students to articulate what they are conscious of already believing but also teaches them about some of the insights that might never otherwise be revealed—to them, to us, or the world—by moving beyond school and into a range of the communities of which they are a part.

The photo walk is never just one walk; it is always a series of strolls and photographic examinations of particular sites, both with and without holding in mind the guiding questions offered. We typically take students on distinct walks in their classrooms and in and around their schools. Then students are assigned photo walks of their own, to be taken anywhere but a school-related context. They are instructed to take a minimum of twenty pictures in each setting, always taking at least two shots of each subject. They take close-ups and more distant shots, visually considering their photographic topics from up high and then down low, shooting blurry and then finely focused images. They are instructed to *never* delete an image; often the best, most compelling, and most honest images are those taken by accident and are not recognized as "good" until the student sits down with someone to discuss it in an elicitation conference.

Students are called upon to take images that they believe explicitly and obviously answer at least one of the TSE questions. (What is the purpose of school? What helps you to attend and be successful in school? What gets in the way of your attendance and success?) They are given permission to take pictures that might serve as metaphorical responses to these queries, photos that seem to have nothing to do with these questions, and images that simply interest them. They are asked to take these series of images—often as many as several hundred—over several rounds of photo walks in a range of contexts, including in settings that they might even complain have nothing to do with their responses. We explain to young people that these are "brain-hurting" activities—exercises whose relevance is not immediately clear but the results of which are, almost without exception, some of the richest and our students' favorites.

Numerous tools are used to provide scaffolding for these walks, including the Photo Walk Planning Tool found in appendix 8.1.

Another specific guideline and tool for conducting and supporting students' engagement with these exercises is the Photo Walk Photo Log, found in appendix 8.2. When we are working with groups larger than our camera inventory, this tool allows students without cameras to participate in the project by making notes on the photos they would have taken.

We engage in these photo walks in part so that youths generate the largest, most expansive pool of images and potential writing topics. Venturing beyond our classroom to provide "real world" contexts for these photo-based writing assignments also serves as a motivating activity for our students. It's a painful reality that these youth often appreciate moving beyond our classroom and school, the primary sites where their negative writing identities have been formed and cemented and where even purposeful work too frequently seems irrelevant.

Perhaps most usefully, these photo walks intrigued our students because they created an even larger space for the incorporation of their lives, families, "families," communities, and voices into our English language arts and writing curricula. Trusting young adolescents to take the project cameras into their homes and neighborhoods allows them to see that many things in their lives have an impact on their successes and failures in our language arts setting. Almost without exception, young people who had previously been challenged to care about writing tasks in our class discovered a greater confidence in their composition skills as a result of letting the outside world be a part of our curriculum. Their engaged and improved writing performance carried over to their increased investment in and success with writing activities throughout the rest of the school year. They repeatedly demonstrated a newfound awareness that they *could* problematize the academic and life challenges they were encountering. They displayed the ability to devise potential solutions to these difficulties and to articulate these orally, in images, and in writing.

"Writing Time Is Not Measured in Forty-Minute Periods"

"No, Thank You."

I have friends who are in gangs, and some of my brother's friends are, too. One day I was in [the library] and I found my brother's friends and they said, "Hi, Lucelly. How are you?" I said, "Fine, thank you." They said, "Do you want to come to my girlfriend's house?" I said "No, thank you." . . . And he got mad and said, "You better come." And I said, "Why?" Then he pushed me down and he said, "Walk." I was crying and he said, "You better be quiet." And I said, "Okay." Then he saw an old man who was walking in the street. When the old man saw us he was walking slow, but then he started walking fast. And my brother's friend pulled out his knife and he said to the old man, "Stop." And the old man stopped. My brother's friend said to the old man, "If you move, you are going to die." . . . I told my brother's friend, "Stop, don't do anything to him. He is an old man." He said, "Be quiet." . . . My brother's friend asked the old man, "Do you have money?" The old man said, "Yes." My brother's friend said, "Give me the money." And the poor man took out his money. And my brother's friend said, "Thank you." My brother's friend said to the old man, "Take off your shoes." The old man said, "No." He said, "I said take off your shoes." The old man said, "Okay." My brother's friend said, "The police are coming. Run, Lucelly!" And I ran fast. —Lucelly

Lucelly was a participant in a middle school language arts class for English-language learners. She socialized well with many of her classmates, and she was friendly and even revealed a mature sense of humor and a wisdom well beyond her thirteen years when interacting with adults. Her performance in our class was uneven; she would often work diligently to complete her assignments, and then other times appear to be unabashedly disengaged. She was a capable English writer, but we did not always see this ability play out with positive results in school.

She flipped an engagement switch when we offered the alternative writing structures and photo-driven activities of TSE. While practically all of the youth took advantage of the chance to share their personal lives through these unique academic tasks, Lucelly dug deepest. She was more engaged in the photo walk activities than perhaps anyone else in class and more so than we had seen her with any other assignment we posed.

Lucelly shared a lot of difficult information, and she did so with a resignation that we both admired and found troubling. She most often revealed painful, occasionally shocking details about her family, including the very traditional gendered role she was required to play and her consciousness of how her academic prospects and family and community expectations for academic achievement were limited as a result. She owned the writing activities we presented in extraordinarily personal ways, seeming to understand for the first time that school could matter to her, if either teachers or students would allow it.

Lucelly's writing and image above were detailed and heart-rending examples of the types of written and photographic responses we have seen from our students—realities we hope that they are better able to understand and that we can now better consider as we work to support their English writing and speaking development. Still learning English after arriving from Guatemala a few years prior, Lucelly committed a considerable amount of time to revising this reflection. But Lucelly's initial engagement did not come easily, and it was from her that we learned one of the most significant lessons about writing instruction that we now enact almost every day.

Like so many of our students, Lucelly "got" school and the writing required in it just enough to be resistant to it: she was capable of writing at least skeletal descriptions of her photographs, but after years of frustrating experiences in

English classes, she had developed a quiet defiance when faced with the "on demand" requirement to do so. While our students often cannot write or do not have sufficient writing efficacy to compose in the moment in the way that school schedules require, this project revealed that if we engaged with young adults over longer periods of time they would find more writing success. Given the lack of writing achievement with which many students were familiar—as well as the number of out-of-school responsibilities with which they were bombarded—they often do not have the mental space or actual time to consider our school writing activities.

For our students, writing time is not, cannot, and should not be measured in forty-minute periods or eighty-five-minute blocks. Students who struggle with writing, with negative writer identities, and with compromised or undeveloped senses of writing efficacy simply cannot perform as writers in these compressed periods, in the face of "on demand" writing tasks. In fact, they are as likely to feign opposition or disinterest when called on to write in these brief, public, spur-of-the-moment ways. But when TSE youth are provided with more one-on-one attention, more time to consider how and what they might write about a given photograph, and a more authentic schedule of drafting and revising, they are considerably more willing to engage and able to find success with our writing tasks.

Students' reflections and images and our TSE project interactions revealed that English teachers might provide youths with extended periods of time to draft and revise their writing efforts, in spite of what more traditional, standardized assessments might demand. These young women and men need compassionate adults who will pay attention to them over time, and listen without discrimination when they are ready to disclose what they are thinking, doing, and failing to understand. Perhaps this is most important when students are ready to write and talk about the highlights and challenges of their family and community and the ways that these are impacting their schooling and writing experiences. If we organized our instruction around more inclusive and responsive structures, over a more extended period of interactions, outside of the artificial limits of our class periods and school schedules, then students might listen to us about the importance of their writing efforts.

Writing For and Sharing With a Community

FIGURE 8.2

"Motivation"

This is a picture of me and my cousin. The reason I chose this is because he is my family and that could be a big factor in me doing well in school. When I think about the things I could do for my family it motivates me. The people that I care about the most help me a lot. My family helps me by staying on you, by asking me a lot about school and trying to help me all the time, and always making sure I'm doing what I'm supposed to do. —Derek

As a sophomore in our English class, Derek seemed to embody the generational disengagement from school that his community had lived and we as veteran teachers had witnessed. His low "D" average across all his classes clearly represented the threat to his ability to obtain a high school diploma. Derek rarely participated in English class, rarely did his homework, and appeared not to study for our assessments, yet he always found a way to barely pass. He appeared to be the epitome of a teacher's nightmare and the enactment of negative stereotypes about urban youth. He seemed to enjoy making wisecracks during those moments in our class meant for reflection and writing, and his peers showed their appreciation for his sarcasm and silliness.

Derek, however, had another side, one that forced us to suspend our assumptions about his abilities and the persona he had forged as a student not cut out for success in school. It turned out that his need for an audience in our class wasn't the problem; it was the solution. It was indicative of the fact that he, like so many of his peers, needed to write for a larger audience, more than just caring and responsive teachers. He was crying out for an authentic audience.

As we examined each of Derek's writing efforts from the project, we noticed that every one focused on family, his aunts, his cousins, and, most frequently, his mother. Through our elicitation conferences with him, we learned of his desire to make life easier for his mom: he wanted to eventually buy her a house and allow her to stop working long hours and days. It was in those momentary exchanges that Derek, a young man who previously appeared to dismiss with a comic flip of the wrist everything we offered, learned that, if he were to achieve his goal of providing for his mother, he would need to become more involved in his schooling.

Derek informed us he did not have any models in his family for doing well in school. He said he wanted to eventually set an example for others in his family. When Derek eventually saw his photos and writing hang in a public exhibition in the city library and then in his high school, he was clearly surprised by his own pride in these displays, as well as by the recognition he received from community members.

The young people in our project regularly revealed deeply personal information about their families and communities. Of course, they often highlighted how these family and community members played explicitly both supportive and obstructive roles in their school and writing lives. They also frequently surprised us, the audiences of our project's exhibitions and publications, and even themselves with the complex and even contrary nature of these roles: who assisted them, who impeded them, and the form these encouragements and obstacles took.

But perhaps the most important insights students revealed were the extent to which they appreciated having a beyond-the-classroom audience for their images and writings—and how surprised they were that such a community existed for their efforts and ideas. This was another lesson of authenticity. Young people who struggle to attend and achieve in school and to complete and find success with writing need audiences who interrupt these writing relationships, identities, and expectations. They need to be almost shocked into an awareness that they can write well, can grow as writers, and that their writing can matter.

Of course, the audiences for whom our high school students write also might include the broad range of adults who influence their lives, relationships to school, and literacy choices. Amanda photographed her grandmother at the local breakfast/lunch counter she managed and where Amanda worked. She described the role her grandmother played in her life and schooling. Amanda's grandmother encouraged her literacy achievement, recognized Amanda for her English class accomplishments, and "sweated the details" when it came to completing English homework, a financial aid application, or writing a college essay.

Each of the TSE projects included public exhibitions of youths' photographs and writings, for which we produced postcards and posters, and for which we eventually devised straightforward templates. Adolescents have shared their efforts in gallery spaces packed with friends, family, school personnel, and members of the community. Sharing their work with broader audiences—often comprised of strangers or people these adolescents barely know, such as the photographers and preservice teachers who assisted us on our many project days—has created important moments for them—as members of society, as artists, as writers, and as social critics.

These exhibitions have introduced us and our students to the notion of "event-ness"—to the idea and practice of taking what is typically just a school product and sharing it via an occasion that suggests their writing and images matter to a much larger pool of people in their communities, that they warrant a happening akin to a celebration or premiere.

As well, the adolescents of our project consistently described and illustrated how they would be more motivated to write if they could share their efforts not only with this expanded community audience. The children our high school students encountered via their numerous part-time jobs also comprised an authentic audience for adolescents' writings and photographs. Reese took an image of a middle school–aged boy at a recreation center where he worked and described how he longed to teach this young man that he should not count on being a professional athlete as his only life option. While Reese regularly played sports with these children, he also urged them to consider the value of school and to pursue their academic responsibilities with the same verve they were committing to hoops. He suggested that image-driven writing about his hopes for these early adolescents' futures might be emphasized in our English classrooms.

The students were most intrigued by opportunities to share their insights, images, and reflections with the younger members of their families and neighborhoods—the children for whom they are often responsible. City high school and middle school students frequently adopt caretaking roles for children to supplement the support provided by adults, the desire to find success in their own lives, and the longing to spare these youngsters the isolation these teens encounter. While we were often focused on the teacher and policymaker audiences for these students' work, the students were compelled to share their projects and perspectives with this barely next generation.

Appendix 8.1

Photo Walk Planning Tool

Name: _____   Date: _____

Idea #1

One picture I want to take would show:

☐ The purpose of school or why I come to school
☐ Things and people that support my success in school
☐ Things and people that get in the way my success in school

What would you take a picture of?
_____

Where would you take this picture?
_____

Describe the picture as you see it in your head:
_____
_____
_____

Idea #2

One picture I want to take would show:

☐ The purpose of school or why I come to school
☐ Things and people that support my success in school
☐ Things and people that get in the way my success in school

What would you take a picture of?
_____

Where would you take this picture?
_____

Describe the picture as you see it in your head:
_____
_____
_____

Idea #3

One picture I want to take would show:

☐ The purpose of school or why I come to school
☐ Things and people that support my success in school
☐ Things and people that get in the way my success in school

What would you take a picture of?
_____

Where would you take this picture?
_____

Describe the picture as you see it in your head:
_____
_____
_____

Appendix 8.2

Photo Walk Photo Log

Name: _____ Date: _____

Photo Walk Location: _____

1. What do you believe are the purposes of school?

2. Who or what supports your success in school? What or who helps you to show up for school? What people IN or OUT of school help you to do well in school?

3. Who or what gets in the way of your success in school? What or who impedes or stops you from attending school? What people IN or OUT of school get in the way of you doing well in school?

Photo #	Questions (1, 2 and/or 3) this picture answers	Description of photograph
1		
2		
3		
4		
5		
6		
7		
8		
9		
10		

Picturing Mentors and Mentoring

FIGURE 9.1

"Make Things Better"

This picture is of my grandmother that I took in front of her job. My grandmother is 71 years old and has worked in childcare for 23 years. She continues to work because she doesn't have any money to retire and money is a constant problem in our house: I feel like if I go to school and work hard someday I can have a good paying job. I want to be able to make things better for her but also my mother. I'm going to school for me and my family. —Andranic

Andranic struggled a bit in Jim's English class, and it became apparent during a summer writing session that she was frustrated with herself and her writing efforts. As she stared at a computer screen, trying to answer one of the project questions, tears welled up in her eyes. She told us how discouraged she was with being unable to concentrate even on an academic task in which she was interested. After a conversation the next week with Andranic's mother, Jim referred Andranic to the school psychologist. She was tested and diagnosed with a learning disability.

Andranic did much better with proper support, not just in Jim's class and with writing, but with school overall. She had a heightened sense of efficacy and new knowledge about what she described as something "broken" within. Andranic's growing confidence only strengthened the clarity of a focus she had held all along: school was going to help her to make a better life for her and for the strong women with whom she lived.

Like so many of our students, Andranic had an adult awareness of the financial challenges her family was facing and a natural longing to improve the conditions of her family members' lives, including the life of her septuagenarian grandmother who had to continue to work full time long after she might have retired. But in our conversations with Andranic, before and after she took the above picture and eventually wrote the accompanying paragraph, we discovered something else that we found both informative and troubling. Andranic not only hoped to "make things better" for her grandma and family; she planned and even expected to address her family's ever-present economic woes, though no one in her world had informed her that she was responsible for doing so. That is, Andranic was ready and willing to play a family leadership and mentoring role for her younger siblings, for her mom, and even for her aging grandmother.

Andranic's story echoed the experience and mentoring activities of many of the TSE project participants: the qualities and identities of the mentors and role models to whom our students looked for their life, school, and writing success were frequently unanticipated, sometimes shocking, and often seemed counterintuitive. Our grand assumptions were challenged about who these youth considered mentors, how they defined mentors and mentoring, which traits made the mentors successful in these exemplar capacities, and whether youth were conscious of the individuals in their lives who served in these supportive roles.

The diverse young women and men in the Through Students' Eyes project count on even those peers and adults in their lives who have failed to find school and worldly success as exemplars who can motivate them—and who they can in turn inspire—to pursue academic, personal, and financial achievement. Of course, this reality has implications for how teachers, school administrators, and the adults in their lives might approach youth, and for how we as English teachers might organize our writing instruction practices. We must all be aware of the ways in which even negative examples of school, life, and writing engagement and attainment can prompt young adults to be more conscious of their own academic and worldly success.

After more than a decade of engaging with youth via TSE, we have discovered a number of mentor- and mentoring-related pedagogical and writing instruction insights that we share in this chapter. These include the practice of Using Others' Images as a Way In and the idea that, as teachers, we must Fake It until You Find It. As well, our most effective writing mentoring activities are rooted in the notion that in our classrooms there can be No Tourists and that we might recognize what we now call the Mentoring Boomerang.

Using Others' Images as a Way In

"The Shoreline"

I love this picture because it speaks to me about life in general. This picture . . . reflects how sometimes I mess up, but by the time I realize it, everything has already been washed away. The waves remind me to let things go and to keep on going because life goes on and on. It also reminds me not to look back to the past because the past is already gone. If I always focus on the past, then I will live in the past and not focus on my future. Even if I make mistakes, I need to focus on how I can fix them and focus on my future. In school, you may sometimes mess up, but I think that is part of the purpose. Sometimes you need to make mistakes and learn from them so that you don't repeat the same mistakes twice. —Selene

Marriam, Selene's language arts teacher, recognized that she needed some new tools and a more engaging orientation to writing instruction if she were going to serve her increasingly diverse, immigrant, and English-language-learning students. Selene was extremely bright and revealed both writing talent and a conscientiousness about her work—but only if she was engaged in the task. As evidenced by the writing above and the accompanying image of one of the many mid-Atlantic coast beaches to which our students have ready summer access, Selene found our writing elicitation project worth her while.

Marriam observed, too, that Selene often put creative spins on the work she did complete in class. But she also became aware of Selene's difficult family situation, and on more than one occasion Selene expressed relief to be at school and away from the tensions at home. Like so many of our diverse and disenfranchised students, Selene often appeared shy and disengaged, but she opened up to the few teachers who she trusted, even admitting that she fervently wanted to go to college.

This ex-urban community had evolved at lightning speed, and Selene's school now consisted of over 40 percent English-language learners. In such a context it is not just the students who are challenged to find success, it is also frequently the veteran English teachers who were trained and had worked almost exclusively with student populations that had very different relationships to writing—and school in general—than the young people now passing through classroom doors. Marriam was intrigued by the photovoice methods of TSE and agreed to work with a small group of young women for one summer project. We all assumed that such a structure—five young women and one teacher, weekly small group and individual sessions, and some nominal but meaningful incentives for the youth to participate—was a recipe for guaranteed success.

But as we have noted, too many of our students and project participants were still new to the culture of US schools and cautious in light of their novice student state. As a result, by the time they reach us in the later middle to high school years, they very reasonably have developed a negative orientation to school and its writing tasks. They may present as defensive or dismissive in class in order to maintain dignity in a situation where they feel inferior. Sometimes none of our methods and no amount of extra effort is sufficient for guiding them toward an appreciation for or success with writing instruction and school. Sometimes—as with Selene—it is only via others'—their peers'—images that they find a "way in" to these writing activities.

Over TSE's first few years, we developed tools through which we could share with our students examples of what other young adults from around the United States and beyond had described and illustrated about their own relationships to school. We drew on images and reflections from these previous versions of the project to call upon adolescents to identify which of the project questions they thought the demonstration pictures were intended to address. We were, of course, aware of the power and even necessity of offering our students models to scaffold them to success in our classrooms. Likewise, we found such exemplars to be mandatory for engaging disenfranchised youth with writing instruction. The young people were motivated by the fact that these images visually represented some of the issues with which they were already concerned and that the images had been taken and chosen by their peers.

Considering their peers' images and interpretations without adult mediation consistently allowed the students to recognize that, while attempting to answer a question with photographs can initially seem like an obtuse activity, considering pictures in this way is, ultimately, a freeing and empowering approach to writing, leaving big and beautiful room for interpretation. Somehow they knew that responding to a question posed to them in words only allowed for one answer—a reply they felt certain they did not know. But responding to a query via consideration of a photograph naturally gave them the space to answer confidently with their own interpretation.

Photograph interpretation and elicitation activities that begin with their peers' pictures and writings also provided youth with something of a brainstorming and writing safety net and with a "way in" to their ideas that they had not discovered previously. For example, while we knew that gangs were a growing concern for the young adults in Selene's community—and an issue with which the previously rural residents, teachers, school and elected leaders, and police were unfamiliar—they appreciated seeing images with which they could readily connect their own experiences and expertise. And often it was only when we shared pictures from other young people encountering similar issues, tensions, and challenges that they felt comfortable articulating and depicting their own.

After considering their peers' images and writings, the TSE project youth frequently surprised us with their uncharacteristic perspectives on what we previously would have considered stereotypical concerns. Perhaps most importantly, these activities tempered that foundational and otherwise impervious writing fear with which so many of our students approached us and their English teachers. We know now that, particularly with writing, our students need to know—to *see*—what is possible and what is expected of them. Such clarity with writing can help to shift their orientations with school itself, leading them to engage and find success with activities and an institution that is often as foreign to them as the new language they are learning.

Of course, it was not just the act of viewing others' images that supported their engagement and success with our project and these writing efforts. It was also opportunities to interact with peers around their images and reflections—a very social exchange—through which they were both more able and more motivated to write. While many English teachers are cautious about these peer interactions and small group projects, considering these to be questionable uses of instructional time, youth are frequently comfortable with these activities and regard them as supportive of life and employment skills. Such group-focused activities also provide adolescents with chances to check their understandings of lesson content with other trusted individuals—their peers—before teachers instruct or assess them.

Fake It Until You Find It

"Only Hope"

In this photo are my god-sister and her nephew. This is an example of what helps you to succeed in school. They have a great relationship, a bond that can't be broken. And when you have people in your life that you know you're an example to, it's only right to set a good one, because you're indeed a cosmic influence on them. Other people's lives are depending on hers, whether she succeeds or fails; they will all be affected by it. So her goal in life is to succeed in all that she does not just for herself but also for those who have no hope. To most of us, it's hard to cast aside our selfishness by choosing to take control over our lives and resist the everyday temptations of this world by standing above the influence. When your mind is made up on what you would and wouldn't do, no one can change your mindset. Then that's when choosing the right people to surround yourself with comes to mind, and you realize that it's much easier when those are people who have the same goals. —Rhandi

Rhandi proved to be one of the most gifted photographers we have encountered in a dozen years of working with TSE projects. We regularly work with highly trained artistic photographers and photojournalists, and we recognize and appreciate that some individuals simply are born with particular talents, aptitudes, and abilities. When a young woman from an impoverished community can capture, through both elaborately staged pictures and spontaneous shots, images that cause the viewer to pause and ponder, it becomes clear that natural photographic aptitude exists. Rhandi surprised herself and her teachers with her artistic, writing, and critical reflective abilities.

Rhandi proved to be not only a gifted photographer but, as demonstrated by the writing above and the accompanying image of her nephew and god-sister, also one who found the photo-elicitation method to be a uniquely effective vehicle for sharing complex perspectives, especially when she was offering insight into the nature of mentors and mentoring in her world. The quality of her writing when she was using images was longer and richer in content than her classroom experiences, and some of the ideas she shared were revelations. It was our experience with her that highlighted one of the most important lessons about effective writing instruction that we have encountered: as teachers we must *fake* it—our unwavering enthusiasm for youths' writings, images, ideas, and potential—until we *find* it.

The harsh teaching truth here is that we had been struggling to connect with Rhandi in our classroom all year long, though we had been diligent about remaining positive with her. On average, classroom teachers work with young people for 180 days across the school year. With block rather than period scheduling, we might see a student for about half this number of class sessions. But even ninety lessons is a lot for any teacher to maintain a level of enthusiasm that will engage and intrigue young people enough that they will read a classic novel or complete a research essay.

Rhandi's affect—whether it was detachment, dismissal, discomfort, distraction, or just dissing—reminded us that we have to muster that passion level with virtually every lesson we teach, with every interaction with the young people with whom we share our classroom, school, and community spaces. Once we begin to present such enthusiasm on a topic or text—even one for which we naturally have little fervor or on a day on which we simply do not have that energy—then, more often than not, it becomes contagious in the classroom. At the least, our students appreciate these persistent efforts to cajole them and win them over.

Older students are often teacher-savvy enough and have a good enough relationship with us to respect and sometimes even playfully mock our efforts to engage them. Fake it until you—and/or your students—*find* it. Fake it until you—and/or your students—*believe* it. Fake it until you *make* it. While the suggestion that a teacher would ever need to "fake" an emotion with students might seem inappropriate to readers who have not spent a significant time in the classroom, we have come to realize that doing so is a completely reasonable and even necessary pedagogical coping strategy.

Rhandi was one who challenged our time-tested, veteran-teacher reserve of such energy and the strategies to share it. She seemed intelligent enough— maybe above average—to be successful in our classroom and with our writing activities. She was world wise and world weary, but did not appear to be so hardened that she could not be reached. But still, across a year, we struggled to find the connection with her that would motivate her to write. We wrestled with how to believe that our methods would ever be effective with Rhandi and, at least on a handful of occasions, we struggled even to fake our energy and persistence.

That is, right up until we invited Rhandi, coaxed her, and initially pleaded with her to participate in a summer version of our project. We played the ultimate "fake it" teacher lottery: we pleaded with a student who seemed to be on the verge of losing interest in school to participate in a project for which she had shown no curiosity, simply because we wanted to have one more opportunity to reach her, because we just did not want to give up even after a year of frustration in our classroom interactions with her.

This is another of the lessons about mentors and mentoring that our students have taught us: the adults in their lives, the ones who really matter, are those who persist, who show up every day, who fake and actually find the faith in young people that might make all the difference in their lives. When we are seeking these models and exemplars for our students, when we are nudging them toward making the healthiest choices about with whom they will surround themselves, our passionate persistence is everything. With enough consistent, daily support for their search for these mentors—again, in forms that we might not understand or appreciate—they will be more likely to consider our guidance.

No Tourists

FIGURE 9.2

"My Uncle Sid"

I think of him as one of my biggest inspirations. He is one of the many people that will sit down with me and talk to me about how important it is to go to school and get a good education. But he doesn't just talk to me about school. He also makes me feel like I can go to him about anything no matter what it may be and he helps me with every thing and any thing. —Raeshaun

Raeshaun—or Rae—was in the video production class at Lincoln-West HS where we first collaborated, and he was a very articulate young man. Rae was popular with the female students and was always sought out for group work by the girls in his classes. Yet Rae was deeply respectful of women, and it was clear that his mom had very intentionally raised him to be so. While many of his male peers defined themselves by the clique or crowd to which they belonged, Rae appeared to live a solitary, self-sufficient life. He presented as easy-going and wise beyond his years—yet another "old soul." College was never a question with Raeshaun; nothing was going to distract him from his goals. We had no doubt he would be successful, and today he is a college graduate, a husband, and a member of the workforce.

Raeshaun's image and reflection above echoed a consistent message about mentors and mentoring: we must allow for broader notions of the exemplars who support young adults in our classes and beyond. Allowing disengaged students to identify these mentors and exemplars is one of the most productive writing activities and one of the most engaging of questions for students.

Rae went one step further and highlighted a notion of "mentoring that matters," which has become foundational to our writing instruction efforts. Rae illustrated and explicitly discussed how, with writing instruction, virtually anyone can play a mentoring role, because almost every person in a youth's life can be an audience for an adolescent's writing efforts. Or, perhaps more accurately, when it comes to writing instruction, everyone in a young person's life *must* play a mentoring role. We sum up this idea with the phrase *No Tourists*.

We enact this No Tourists notion in numerous ways in our classroom and around our writing instruction. We discussed in chapter 4 how on almost every first class day of each new school year and each first day of the Through Students' Eyes project we lead students in the Community Handshake activity and also have momentary one-on-one conferences with each young person, taking pictures of them, introducing ourselves, posing some initial personal query to them, and using these exchanges as a foundation for the relationships we work to build. But such activities are difficult to complete—not to mention conduct—when we are the only teacher in a classroom of thirty or so adolescents.

As we noted in chapter 7 when we described our Just Ten Minutes strategy, at moments like these we appeal to almost any responsible adult to help us maintain a productive atmosphere—a team-teaching special education or English as second language colleague, a parade of colleagues who have a planning period and with whom we can trade off such "coverage" favors, a roaming and willing administrator, an instructional aide. We know that our best writing instruction efforts occur in these intimate interactions, but our school, project, and classroom structures—and even some teacher and school personnel labor agreements—do not typically allow for these. A No Tourists orientation allows us to consider alternatives and to find the support we and our students need to implement these one-to-one structures.

We also have learned—in part because of our boundary-spanning roles as university-based and school-based teacher educators—that local colleges of education are often desperate to place their teacher candidates in local high school classrooms for required fieldwork and internships. These individuals are almost universally intelligent, energetic, committed, principled, and *free*—the ideal everyday mentors for our students and the perfect coteachers, even for a day, who can either engage with our students to support their writing activities or who can lead enough of a lesson that we can implement more of those one-to-one structures.

Of course, we are explicit with our students and project participants about this No Tourists notion—we explain on day one, even minute one, that there will be many other caring adults in our classroom or project space, that we expect these young adults to be kind and receptive to our visitors, that they will be present in order to support and challenge our students. We similarly explain to these myriad in-the-moment mentors—the antitourists—that we consider it a privilege to work with our students—to learn about these youths' lives and to learn about how to teach, primarily about writing instruction, via these interactions.

But this No Tourists idea also extends into another practice. We have described earlier in this chapter how these youth look to an often-unexpected pool of family and community members as some of the best mentors outside of school. But we have learned that these exemplars—even the just-older siblings who might have rejected school but are still convinced of and even preachy about its value to these youths—are some of the best writing mentors inside our classrooms.

These family and community members can be some of the best listeners and audience members for our students' writings. They can be diligent elicitation interviewers, very conscientiously querying our students about the images they have taken and the reflections they have drafted. Their presence in our classrooms helps to bridge that school/community divide and enhances the relationships we are trying to build with these youth. Their even occasional presence can be shocking to our students, but for young people who too often have well-established, negative relationships to writing, such jolts can be useful. And even life changing.

The Mentoring Boomerang

"Leader"

This is a picture of my brother and he taught me everything I need to know about school and life. Most of all, my brother shows me how to be a leader, particularly in school. He is there to pick up the slack when my mom drops it and he is a great brother. But when it comes down to school and my books, he constantly stays on me and teaches me to do the same for my younger brother. He means everything to me because all of my life, he's the only person that's really been there for me. He got his GED, but he really wants to see me get my diploma. He is the most important factor in my life. I think kids need role models because they need someone to set the standard on what they could be doing. My brother sets the standard by providing for his girlfriend, my mom, my little brother and me. He is very smart and this shows me that it's possible to put your mind to anything and accomplish it. —Marcus

Marcus's maturity level was at once endearing and maddening. One day he would express himself through bodily sounds and odors to the amusement of his male peers, and the next he would ask if he could record a compelling rap and video about *The Crucible*, which we were reading in class, to demonstrate an almost profound understanding of this text.

Marcus was also a gifted poet with a college-level vocabulary at his disposal. His peers respected him for this talent, and at times this admiration went to his head. We had many conversations about his rapper persona, "KickFlip B," and Marcus frequently mentioned his personal need to not lower the bar for his lyrics. He said, "I don't want to dumb it down. I want people to respect me for who I am." We joked that he would be a rapper for the intellectual crowd. He once had an opportunity to perform at LeBron James's birthday party. It was a black tie event, so we loaned him $150 to rent a tuxedo, telling him it was an investment in his future. Marcus, last we heard and saw, was still trying to make it big in the music/entertainment industry.

With an image of his brother—who at that point had only earned a GED—Marcus spoke explicitly to the ways in which even a high school dropout could serve as a very tangible motivator for youths' school engagement and achievement. His photograph and description suggest that there are exemplars in these youths' lives to whom school leaders should be appealing, but too often these guides are looking for models who exemplify success in the most obvious and explicit ways rather than understanding that these young adults can appreciate constructive lessons in the complexity of these mentors' lives.

The most consistent theme about mentors and mentoring that our students and TSE project participants have described relates to the expanded nature and identity of these exemplars of which we, as their English and writing teachers, must be aware. They are also looking for their teachers, administrators, and virtually every adult in their schools and communities to both be willing to serve in these more complex modeling roles and to support the development of networks of mentors, both in and out of school. They are calling on their teachers to be aware of the details of their lives and of the ways in which even negative examples of school and writing engagement and success can help them to become better students, family members, and even models for their peers. Many highlighted the constructive examples that the adults in their lives provide, in an instructive or even confrontational manner, reminding us how often we fail to recognize these positive models.

Via their photo-elicitation projects and reflective writings, these youths were, in fact, doing something much more than identifying such exemplars and reminding us that we need to expand our consideration of this pool of role models. They often took us a step further, suggesting that part of their English and writing instruction should be the development of a student-generated and facilitated curriculum through which they serve as teachers and mentors to their peers. They longed to instruct their classmates and community members in the science and art of finding a mentor and of working through the often very adult challenges that frame their lives.

The most unexpected mentors these young people identified were, in fact, themselves. Even the youths who were largely disengaged from and unsuccessful in school and with our writing activities believed they could be exemplars for their peers, their younger and older siblings, and even the adult family members. Engaging as role models and developing a mentoring curriculum represented what they considered a profoundly authentic composition task and a starting point for deeper engagement with other school and writing activities. This reflexive, responsive notion and practice of diverse, often disenfranchised youth engaging as mentors for these varied members of their families, communities, and peer networks and even formally assisting with the construction of mentoring lessons represents what we now call the Mentoring Boomerang.

Echoing our No Tourists notion, these young adults also advocated for bringing the peers, family, and community members who are serving as examples to them into their school lives and making them a part of the school curricula. Marcus and so many other youths suggested that our English class structures and our writing instruction activities might support programs that engage adolescents and their families in mentoring activities that explicitly serve both city students and the adults in their lives. These young people should be writing mentors for their peers not because they will share the best writing strategies with their contemporaries or because they will offer the best examples of quality writing to their peers, but because their peers and the members of their families and communities need models of engaged writing and exemplars they can trust. They need a clearer sense of writing efficacy (and to eschew their negative writing identities) that can likely only or best be developed through their engagement with their classmates, friends, and community members. They need better, stronger, safer writing relationships—connections through which they give and relationships that give back.

Conclusion

Even after years of working with young people in some of the most difficult circumstances in urban and ex-urban contexts in the United States, we have to remind ourselves that we cannot allow our potential—and sometimes very reasonable—frustrations with these youths' stances on school and writing to deter us from trying to serve them well. It does not matter if they appear or even are apathetic or oppositional. Our job is the same regardless of the reasons behind our students' apparent or real disengagement from our writing tasks and school in general. We can be some of the ultimate models and mentors for them in their development of healthy relationships to school and writing, and we must maintain a vigilant faith in their ability to engage and be successful. More importantly, they can be the subjects and objects, the givers and receivers, of writing mentoring practices.

We understand now just how much work we have to do to heal the writing relationships our students and TSE project participants already have. This relationship notion of writing instruction is risky, as it requires us to accept that these youths' appreciation for writing—manifested as a result of them composing about things that might have troubled us or seemed questionably relevant to a standard English curricula—would carry over to future, more traditional writings and school in general.

While we as teachers may not be conscious of the complexity of the mentoring activities and mentors' roles in students' lives, their peers, friends, and family and community members are often aware of the convoluted nature of the positions they occupy. This awareness appears to make these individuals more efficient and effective leaders, as they have too often known mostly failure with our writing activities and in our English classes and schools, but they appreciate the obligation they have to persuade the young people whose lives they impact not to follow this course. Again, our writing instruction practices might be the best means through which youth and teachers can identify the often negative assumptions made about who might serve as the most effective role models.

Appendix 9.1

Name: _____   Date: _____

Reading Images

Consider the photographs below as potential answers to the project questions, then decide which question you
think each image addresses. Each of these was taken by another youth who participated in the project.
A picture may answer more than one of the project questions. Explain your choice(s) with details and examples.

Photograph A answers the following question(s):

❑ What is the purpose of school?

❑ What supports your success in school?

❑ What things get in the way of your success in school?

What evidence supports your answer?

> *Teacher:*
> *Insert photo A here*

_____

_____

_____

_____

_____

Photograph B answers the following question(s):

❑ What is the purpose of school?

❑ What supports your success in school?

❑ What things get in the way of your success in school?

What evidence supports your answer?

> *Teacher:*
> *Insert photo B here*

_____

_____

_____

_____

_____

Photograph C answers the following question(s):

❏ What is the purpose of school?

❏ What supports your success in school?

❏ What things get in the way of your success in school?

What evidence supports your answer?

> *Teacher:*
> *Insert photo C here*

The Bigger Picture: Discuss these questions with your peers

Which photograph(s) answered more than one question? Discuss why you chose the questions you did.

How did the way you think about school change as a result of looking at these photographs?

What new answers have you generated to the project questions?

Picturing Success and Failure

FIGURE 10.1

"Mobile Home"

This picture that I've taken is called Mobile Home and it represents the purpose of school for me. The reason why this picture is my purpose of being in school is, I don't want to grow up to be a homeless person. I want to set a strong and stable foundation for my family and live in a nice wonderful home, that's safe for me and my family and the way I'm going to start building that foundation is to finish school and go to college. —Eon

Behind Eon's dramatic comic/tragic facade, he was a brilliant young man with a dangerously short fuse. Eon was often on a mission to prove that he was far more than what you might assume about him, and he would challenge his peers' often innocently negative feedback about his writing with extreme anger. Indeed, it seemed Eon felt persecuted by his perception that very few people in his life really knew who he was, yet he often impeded others' abilities to do so because he was so judgmental and selective about who would be allowed into his world.

As we grew to genuinely appreciate Eon's sarcastic and tongue-in-cheek humor, we often feared that his lack of impulse control would eventually get him into serious trouble; he had no qualms with being angrily aggressive with his peers and teachers alike, often for slights only he perceived. It was only when we read the reflection on the image above that we began to understand the source of his fury: he felt a deep-seated fear and insecurity that was rooted in the transience of his home life.

Of course, having knowledge of a youth's anxieties did not translate to being prepared for the sudden, almost inexplicable explosions that were occasionally the result. We remember an incident in class when Eon had to be physically restrained by another of our students and TSE project participants from starting a fistfight with a female student who Eon had felt disrespected him. "You don't know me! You don't know me!" he repeatedly yelled as he tried to close the distance between himself and the unsuspecting young woman who was the subject of his rage. Our solution to serving Eon better as his English and writing teachers, to getting to know him differently and better, and to helping to make a richer and more proactive sense of his anger and pain was to invite him to participate in TSE.

The project opportunity clearly helped Eon—and us and his peers and the audiences of his photographic and written work—appreciate the life-or-death, safe-or-threatened, having-a-home-or-homeless perspective from which he was operating. His image and reflection illustrate both the subject matter of our students' thinking about success and failure and, perhaps even more importantly, the fact that they so often consider their own well-being and the obstacles they face. Our young people are painfully aware of the challenging paths they face. Yet when given a chance to explore these topics via the rich photo-elicitation methods we use, they reveal that they are anything but apathetic about school and their futures.

This final chapter highlights some of the notions of "success" and "failure" that our students and TSE project participants have depicted and described over the years of our work with them. We share a final collection of youths' images and reflections to illustrate these ideas, again linking them to some of the foundational writing instruction principles and practices that guide our work. These include the notion and orientation of a Stance of Humility and Invitation and the idea that we should never use Drive-By Assessments. They also include the practice of evaluating our students' writing through both Local and Global Assessments, and the notion that our students' writing efforts are never done—they're just due.

Stance of Humility and Invitation

FIGURE 10.2

"The Exact Moment"

This picture shows my best friend, Jerome, jumping off the stage at my church. He was practicing a dance routine and preparing for the Youth Explosion that was coming up. This picture shows his determination and practice while he was running then jumping off the stage. I wanted to get his picture, but couldn't capture him in midair. He kept getting mad but ended up doing it over and over again until we finally got this action shot. This proves that even frustration should not get in the way of doing what you want, love and enjoy. Sometimes life gets frustrating and not giving up and persevering will lead to success. The will to do more than you're supposed to or going over and above, as shown in this picture, illustrates that determination helps you get far whether it is at church or in school. —Tamara

Tamara was one of those city youth who—as if by merely existing—gave people the wrong impression. She was a stout, young African American woman, somewhat imposing by her physical stature alone. She also had that stereotypical hardened look about her—the facial expression that too many people who don't know city kids, and especially African American adolescents, assume is an indication of their cold-hearted indifference toward school, the people they meet, and life in general. If you met her on the street or had a chance just to study a picture of her face, you'd think she was perhaps as much as a decade older than she actually was.

But Tamara's story was actually much more complicated than these impressions would allow us to appreciate. She was a voracious reader, a talented writer, and a mile-a-minute talker with a rapid-fire delivery that often made it nearly impossible to understand what she was saying, especially for her teachers, who struggled to bridge what seemed a large cultural gap. Of course, it was not unusual for us and our teaching peers to struggle to understand the speech patterns and even vocabulary of the occasional student. But with Tamara, everyone she encountered in class had difficulty understanding her speech—to the point that we considered recommending to her counselor that she see a speech therapist.

While we often felt as if we were challenged to communicate with Tamara, this did not stop us from developing a strong affinity for her, which was reciprocated. She came to spend a great deal of time in Jim's room outside of our tenth-grade English class, frequently escaping from the cafeteria to camp out with us for the latter half of her lunch period. It did not seem to matter what we were doing during these regular visits; while she was her usual stone-faced self, she clearly appreciated our company, and stoically welcomed the adult attention, maybe filling the void of maturity she felt when she was surrounded by her peers.

We also remember Tamara fondly—and painfully—for a few other reasons. She had the most potent, hand-numbing "high five" of any student we have ever met of either gender. We also recall Tamara because she became a star in Jim's classroom and in our project. She never needed to advertise the fact that she was engaging deeply with daily homework assignments or taking and writing about photographs with the most serious and thoughtful of intent. She just showed up consistently and wrote some of the most insightful reflections to describe some of the most intentionally shot and selected pictures.

We also recollect a particular day in class that she showed rare emotion. She was upset because her grandmother had punished her because she thought Tamara was lying about where she had been the night before. "I told her I had to catch the bus to go visit my mom downtown. She don't believe me. Why would I lie about something like that?"

We asked Tamara where her mom lived downtown.

She fired off an answer and an explanation and a query in a split second. "In a nursing home. She had a stroke and had brain surgery. She really doesn't even know I'm there, but that's cool. I just read to her and talk to her or sometimes just watch TV with her. Want to see a picture of her?"

In Tamara's mind, this was, of course, a rhetorical question. She flipped open her cellphone, deftly navigated the technology, and offered us a picture of her and her mom. It was a selfie taken by Tamara as she leaned into her mother on her hospital bed. Tamara was absolutely beaming, while her mom peered past the camera with a vacant stare. It was clear from the picture that the brain surgery had left her mother in a borderline vegetative state.

We were saddened but not surprised by how deeply misunderstood she was by her teachers, largely the result of her verbal-assault style of delivery. And yet, there she was, on a random project Saturday, not only telling us about perseverance, but also modeling it for her peers in ways that would undoubtedly earn their respect. Had she ever been given the chance to share such insights—and herself? Had she ever felt comfortable doing so? Our elicitation conferences provided us not only with the opportunity to get to know our students better but also to let them make sense of themselves in the context of their own and their peers' world.

These image-focused writing conferences offered us a new perspective on Tamara, her depth of intelligence, and her writing abilities. When we met with her one on one and asked about the photographs she had taken in response to the project questions, she again revealed so much more than her gruff, almost brutish, interactions in our class. She was completely attentive, even hungry, when we sat with her and asked elicitation questions. Then she would take the sometimes rambling notes we kept on these conferences and turn them into lengthy, fluent, wisdom-filled sentences.

The most important writing instruction lesson we drew from our work with Tamara is actually an extension of the One-on-One or Not at All insight detailed in chapter 7. While we were initially reluctant, cautious, even apprehensive to engage in these conferences with Tamara, we nudged ourselves to do so. We were sure to sit next to her, desk by desk, rather than listening to her interpretations of her images while we sat across from her or even stood near her. When she was working on writing revisions and time did not allow us to pull up a desk and spend a more concentrated period with her, we would crouch for a few minutes next to her desk, intentionally positioning our heads several degrees below hers.

When we have the opportunity to share our writing instruction methods with future and other veteran teachers, we often frame these strategies and ask teachers to evaluate them with the question of "What do we have to lose?"—as in, "What do we have to lose by trying out this particular strategy?" The answer—almost without exception—is nothing. We have nothing to lose by sitting next to our students, at what might be perceived as almost inappropriately and intimately close distances, and we have nothing to lose by squatting next to the reluctant writers who are the TSE participants when we are working to engage with them momentarily around their writing efforts. Nothing to lose and everything to gain.

We are our most effective writing instructors, and our students are their most engaged as writers—willing and able to develop as writers—when we approach students with these stances of humility and invitation. We call these "stances" because they are rooted in physical interactions, in the positions of our bodies and those of our students. These young people are almost universally taken aback by our proximity, and they are frequently unsure about how to respond. We cannot suggest that they react with welcoming attitudes, but they appreciate—silently, of course—that we are interacting with them in these respectful, unusual ways.

Perhaps these stances are so important—and so effective—because our students are so accustomed to being approached in other, generally less reverent and deferential ways, by their teachers and other adults. Maybe these physical placements are so much more important with writing activities because these are so absolutely personal, and should be treated with almost churchlike respect. It could be that these conference and crouching positions are so necessary because so many of our youth lack strong, positive senses of writing efficacy. In fact, we have never asked our students and TSE project participants about the utility of the stances with which we approach them, but we know that we have *nothing* to lose and *everything* to gain by daring to carry ourselves in these humble ways.

No Drive-By Writing Assessments

FIGURE 10.3

"Family Signs"

This is a picture of my cousin, D'Angelo. . . . He is throwing up the "King-Kennedy" sign because he represents King-Kennedy. People join gangs because they want to get back at other people who jumped their friends. His mother was born at King-Kennedy. . . . My little brother goes to school right near [these] projects. [I] don't want to join a gang because when gangs start fighting and then you have to represent your 'hood, then people start shooting . . . and then you'll get shot, and you'll think, "I shouldn't have joined that gang." —Allen

Allen might have been all of eight years old when he found his way into the gallery where we conducted our first version of the Through Students' Eyes project. He was a precocious young man—a young boy, really, but one with an awareness of the world that belied his tender years. Allen and his young siblings and the clan of kids who lived in their public housing development just across the street had nowhere else to play but in the hard-packed dirt yard around their buildings. We assume that Allen noticed the steady stream of young adults heading into the gallery every other Saturday during that first summer and investigated in part because he simply wanted something else, something more, to do.

Eventually we supplied Allen with a camera, and he came to join us on these meeting Saturdays. He reminded us that so many of the youth in our communities who may be almost completely disengaged from school are actually just seeking meaningful activities in their lives. Sometimes all it takes to get them interested in very constructive endeavors is to detach these from school and show them that the older youths in their communities are involved. It doesn't hurt to offer a bit of food to get them in the door.

While Allen's instincts drew him into the project and he presented as something of a little old man, his images and the topics he discussed were, not surprisingly, always literal in nature. We were struck by the picture and reflection above; while it depicts and details a common subject of gangs and violence, it was shocking to see a little boy—a child even younger than Allen—"representing" the gang affiliation that was already so familiar to him. This photo echoed the insight above about youths' hunger for constructive activities, but we share it here because of the notion of "drive-by" attacks that were then such a concern in our students' and project youths' neighborhoods.

Our assessments of students' writing should be anything but "drive-by." They should not be random, solitary, and isolated from the contexts in which this writing was completed. We use a silly example of a "drive-by" evaluation of a lengthy marriage to illustrate just how absurd so many of our writing assessment practices are, and what the alternatives might be.

Jim and his wife, Karen, are approaching their twentieth year of marriage. Their family members and friends, including Kristien, would likely and accurately say that their union has never been stronger.

But imagine if, instead of considering their nearly two decades of ups and downs and ups, instead of weighing every bit of evidence of the nature of their partnership, someone determined that next Tuesday at 10:07 a.m. a summative and final evaluation of their marriage would be made, absent of context, ignoring the previous nearly seven thousand days of what may have been marital bliss, and just pulling a day and time—out of a hat. Suppose our society deemed that this was the most accurate, effective, and certainly most efficient method of judging a marriage, and then determined that the future of every union would be determined through such a random assessment.

Such a method of marriage evaluation proposed by a policymaker would be ridiculous. But this is almost precisely the parallel type of writing assessment that teachers perform every day and that are increasingly being demanded of them by state and federal policies: random, in a moment, based on one grossly insufficient piece of evidence, and lacking in any depth or validity.

Assessments of our students' and TSE participants' writing must be rooted, instead, in that notion of "relationship": youths' evolving relationships to writing and their relationships to us, their teachers. We would never assess the stability or quality of a marriage based on one single interaction or one moment, so we must be very careful not to evaluate our students' writing efforts in this high-stakes, snapshot, "drive-by" manner. The relationships that we develop with our students to support their writing and school engagement and their relationships to writing do not occur on a neat schedule. They are as complex as Allen's cousin's relationships to the gangs that were a part of his community, of his family. Our writing assessment methods and the writing achievement ends we expect of our students should never be considered via a single lens, on a single day, on a rigid and unresponsive schedule.

Local and Global Writing Assessment

"Cutting"

When teens cut themselves it's because they're dealing with stress and have self-esteem issues and cutting their arm or wrist has become a very popular way to release this stress. The person in the photo is 13, and we used food coloring for this photo, but she has cut herself before. I think she has two sides: one she shows to everyone as happy. The other side is a person who has problems with her parents: they don't really trust her. Even though I don't cut myself I do deal with a lot of stress and face self-issues. I chose this image because it represents these problems. Dealing with these issues interferes with my school work sometimes and they even make me feel like school is not somewhere I want to be, but I try to find positive ways to release this stress because I know that school is somewhere I need to be. The girl in the photo had a chance to finally have a conversation with her parents and they have gotten more involved in her life. She's a happier person now because she's able to gain their trust back and spends more time with them. —Uniqua

Uniqua—or "Nikki" as she preferred to be called—was a happy, confident, yet occasionally and inexplicably quiet sophomore in Jim's English class at Euclid High School. A cheerleader, Nikki was a student who seemed to prefer to "skate" through class rather than even feign interest in the writing assignments and texts we were presenting to her. Nikki appreciated school for the social opportunities it offered, but was a reluctant participant otherwise. She was also a pretty young lady, and bubbly enough to be a spirit leader, which she happily showed off by modeling her Euclid cheerleader outfit every game day for our English class.

It would be easy to assume that Nikki was more concerned with her physical appearance and others' perceptions of her than with academic achievement or seriously considering the writing assignments doled out by her teachers. We were shocked out of many of the assumptions we had made about Nikki when she shared the staged photograph of one of her classmate's "bloody" forearms that accompanied her writing above. She practiced some of the unwritten rules of "doing school" that were nothing short of a mystery to her generally oblivious and disengaged peers: she knew to be polite, to make eye contact with and smile at adults, and never to rock the proverbial class boat. But Nikki's image and writing revealed a complexity about her that our school and writing instruction structures had not seemed to make space for previously.

Nikki was like so many of our students and TSE project participants: if you considered her behavior and performance on any one day, you might judge her to be a young woman who had decided to disengage almost entirely from school and its writing activities. Someone beyond repair, someone teachers should not waste their time attempting to reach. This would be the easy answer—for us as teachers and for these youth, who often have struggled so much in school and with our writing assignments that it's much safer for them just to give up, sometimes even with deceptive smiles on their faces.

The same could be said of her writing. If someone had so much as glanced at a single example of her writing prior to her participation in Through Students' Eyes, they would have deemed her unworthy of any further writing instruction assistance. We are reminded, again, of the extent to which youths' writing identities have been established by the time they reach us in high school, and how final their relationships to writing seem—unwittingly—to them and to us.

We know now that the only way to begin to work against these identities and relationships and to move youth toward more positive orientations toward writing is via small steps and what we call "local" writing assessments. In both whole-group writing instruction and in the writing conferences we conduct as often as possible, we focus on a single piece of youths' writing and a single element of students' writing, such as word choice, conventions, or voice. While youth may be anxious to improve multiple features of their writing, their writing efficacy is best improved via our laserlike focus on just one component of their compositions.

These writing assessments are "local," too, in the sense that they are conducted with just one student and one teacher or caring adult. While some subjects can be taught in larger group settings—and some of our writing instruction occurs in this mode—this is not the case with the teaching of writing, particularly for youth who are disengaged from school and its writing tasks. Of course, such "local"—one-on-one—writing instruction requires not just a teacher's commitment to engaging with students in this intimate manner; it also calls on us as teachers and teacher educators to advocate for school and classroom structures that allow for such methods. To be the sort of writing instruction teacher our diverse, often immigrant, and too often disenfranchised youth need, teachers must be both guides and advocates.

After we have worked with youth over some length of time—the course of several weeks of our project or across several writing assignments in our classrooms—we also use these one-to-one writing conference structures to conduct "global" writing assessments. This is where we consider that single writing element or our own or one of a student's writing goals over at least two examples of a young person's writing and discuss the evidence of their growth and the future development on which they might concentrate. Writing teachers commonly recognize such "global" evaluations as key structures, yet they are difficult to implement—again, mostly due to the time and classroom structures they require.

We could, of course, look across these multiple examples of students' writing ourselves, sharing our observations and assessments with youth in a summary report that they read, consume, and attempt to respond to with future composition efforts. But after years of working with youth who have found little success with writing, we know that it is infinitely more important that they are aware of—and can articulate—the nature of their writing growth than it is that we—their teachers—can describe this growth and their goals. Such a belief flies in the face of the "objective," high-stakes assessments that are so common in our schools now. But these local and global assessments are intended to offer youth not just opportunities for writing success in our classes or in the short-term Through Students' Eyes project, but chances for achievement and the longer-term development of positive writing identities and efficacy.

Due, Not Done

"Clutter"

This picture represents the "clutter." It shows that there is so much to deal with in life, so many distractions. I think this is what discourages people from education. For example, for my brother Brandon, sports is like a double-edged sword. He gets so caught up in it that sometimes I'd worry that he doesn't care too much about his grades or getting his homework done. But at the same time, it's like a motivation for him. School represents something that can never be taken away from you, something that you can never lose; it's like your own treasure that no one can touch. My parents taught me this—with my mother and my father not going to college, and the way they raised us is that we deserved better as long as we worked for it. —Tim

Tim was one of the first TSE participants from Lincoln-West High School, and he was noticeably, visibly, different from his mostly Latino and African American peers. Despite being a White male, Tim had no problem fitting right in and still maintaining his sense of self. At Lincoln-West the White students were a pronounced minority. That was one of the strengths of the place: it was a United Nations of Cleveland high schools. So many languages, so many cultures and subcultures, so many differences, that it was probably easier for kids to feel completely comfortable in their own, widely varying in shade, skin.

Tim was simultaneously self-possessed and decidedly reserved. And as the writing above about a photograph of his messy bedroom suggests, he had many well-formulated and wise-beyond-his-years opinions about life, education, politics, and art, which we would share when properly queried. He was always willing to have a discussion on a level many of his peers did not appear to fathom. And while some like Tim might have taken abuse from their classmates who perceive such absolute school engagement as a weakness in diverse city contexts where school success seems to be undervalued, Tim was well respected by students and teachers alike.

Interestingly, Tim had managed to fly under the radar in this extraordinarily diverse setting, though he was a whole-heartedly unique character. On his Facebook profile, Tim describes himself in the following way:

> A Minimalist, Cosmonaut, comic nerd, gamer, observer, indecisive, intuitive, logical, artist, tech junkie, an amalgam of experiences. I spend most of my time pondering Schrodinger's Cat, the mysteries of the universe, and how your left lung is smaller than your right lung in order to make room for the heart. This is who I am. I'm what happens when Spock and Zach Morris combine forces. I aim to be a modern day Charles Bukowski. A young Anthony Bourdain. The Hunter S. Thompson of the digital age.

You wouldn't think a young man like this could get lost in any shuffle. As his teachers, it was easy to see how someone like him might be overlooked in most of his classes. He was respectful, polite, earned above average though not exceptional grades, and presented as considerably more mature than many of his peers. Yet he was precisely the kind of student who was too often marginalized in our city school, falling through the cracks and not challenged often enough because every one of his teachers silently assumed that he would, almost regardless of his experiences in our classrooms, be "okay."

We were struck again by Tim's school circumstances when we reviewed the image and writing above. The notion of "clutter" is so relevant to our diverse youth and their school and writing lives. They are simply dealing with so many experiences in their English classes that have steered them down a path that, it seems to us now, could result in the negative writing relationships they have and the rehearsed, dismissive attitudes they share. Somehow we as writing teachers must find a way through these experiences and these relationships, with youth by our sides, and trust that they will find a more positive connection to writing after they have encountered some of the writing instruction methods we have described.

One of the biggest mistakes we make as writing teachers is failing to communicate to students that our writing projects and their writing growth are never done—they're just *due*. Too often our students aim for writing perfection, and they almost invariably fail, given their negative writing relationships and years of frustration in our classes. These youth do not need additional pressure to perform, on demand, with these writing tasks. They do not need additional high-stakes expectations to write and grow.

Rather, they require a developmental orientation to their writing growth. They need their teachers to forgive their writing struggles and to look past their limited writing success. They need to be patient with themselves, encouraged and allowed to have this patience in our classes, with their writing efforts, and the development of their more positive writing identities. As we have noted throughout this volume, writing is always that personal; it is always synonymous with one's sense of self.

References

Ajayi, Lasisi. 2009. English as a second language learners' exploration of multimodal texts in a junior high school. *Journal of Adolescent and Adult Literacy* 52 (7): 585–95.

Alexander, Karl L., Doris R. Entwisle, and Nader S. Kabbani. 2001. The dropout process in life course perspective: Early risk factors at home and school. *Teachers College Record* 103 (5): 760–822.

Alvermann, Donna, and Dorothy S. Strickland. 2004. *Bridging the literacy achievement gap: Grades 4–12.* New York: Teachers College Press.

Anyon, Jean. 1997. *Ghetto schooling: A political economy of urban educational reform.* New York: Teachers College Press.

———. 2005. *Radical possibilities: Public policy, urban education, and a new social movement.* New York: Routledge.

———. 2006. Social class, school knowledge, and the hidden curriculum revisited. In *The new sociology of knowledge*, Lois Weiss and Greg Dimitriadis, eds. New York: Routledge.

Ayala, Jennifer, and Anne Galletta. 2009. Student narratives on relationship, learning, and change in comprehensives turned "small." *Theory into Practice* 48 (3): 198–212.

Balfantz, Robert, and Nettie Legters. 2004. *Locating the dropout crisis: Which high schools produce the nation's dropouts? Where are they located? Who attends them?* Baltimore, MD: Center for Social Organization of Schools, Johns Hopkins University.

Barton, Paul E. 2005. *One-third of a nation: Rising dropout rates and declining opportunities.* Princeton, NJ: Educational Testing Service.

Bell, Athena, Kristien Zenkov, Marriam Ewaida, and Megan Lynch. 2011. Seeing students' perspectives on "quality" teaching: Middle school English language learners' pictures and "at risk" high school youths' voices. *Voices from the Middle* 19 (1): 32–40.

Bell, Shannon. 2008. Photovoice as a strategy for community organizing in the central Appalachian coalfields. *Journal of Appalachian Studies* 14 (1–2): 34–48.

Bondy, Elizabeth, Dorene D. Ross, Caitlin Gallingane, and Elyse Hambacher. 2007. Creating environments of success and resilience: Culturally responsive classroom management. *Urban Education* 42 (4): 326–48.

Boutte, Gloria S., and Edward L. Hill. 2006. African American communities: Implications for culturally relevant teaching. *The New Educator* 2 (4): 311–29.

Bridgeland, John M., John J. Dilulio, and Karen Burke Morison. 2006. *The silent epidemic: Perspectives of high school dropouts.* Washington, DC: Civic Enterprises.

Carlo, Fernando, Antoine Powell, Laura Vazquez, Shoshana Daniels, Clay Smith, Kavitha Mediratta, and Amy Zimmer. 2005. Youth take the lead on high school reform issues: Sistas and Brothas United. *Rethinking Schools* 19 (4): 62.

Christenbury, Leila, Randy Bomer, and Peter Smagorinsky (Eds.). 2009. *Handbook of adolescent literacy research.* New York: Guilford Press.

Connolly, Evelyn, and Gunther Kress. 2011. *The incorporation of multimedia and multimodal learning tools into the teaching of research: A case study of digital storytelling in a high school English class.* New York: Edwin-Mellen.

Cook-Sather, Alison. 2009. *Learning from the student's perspective: A sourcebook for effective teaching.* Boulder, CO: Paradigm Publishers.

Cruz, Barbara, and Stephen Thornton. 2013. *Teaching social studies to English language learners.* 2nd ed. New York: Routledge.

DeFur, Sharon, and Lori Korinek. 2009. Listening to student voices. *Clearing House* 83 (1): 15–19.

Doda, Nancy, and Trudy Knowles. 2008. Listening to the voices of young adolescents. *Middle School Journal* 39 (3): 26–33.

Duncan-Andrade, Jeff. 2006. Urban youth, media literacy, and increased critical civic participation. In *Beyond resistance!: Youth activism and community change—*

New democratic possibilities for practice and policy for America's youth, Pedro Noguera, Shawn A. Ginwright, and Julio Cammarota, eds. New York: Routledge.

Easton, Lois, and Daniel Condon. 2009. A school-wide model for student voice in curriculum development and teacher preparation. In *Learning from the student's perspective: A sourcebook for effective teaching*, Alison Cook-Sather, ed. Boulder, CO: Paradigm Press, 176–93.

Edwards, Patricia, Jennifer Dandridge, Gwendolyn T. McMillon, and Heather M. Pleasants. 2001. Taking ownership of literacy: Who has the power? In *Reconceptualizing literacy in the new age of multiculturalism and pluralism*, Patricia R. Schmidt and Peter B. Mosenthal, eds. Greenwich, CT: Information Age, 111–34.

Erickson, Frederick, Rishi Bagrodia, Alison Cook-Sather, Manuel Espinoza, Susan Jurow, Jeffrey J. Shultz, and Joi Spencer. 2007. Students' experiences of school curriculum: The everyday circumstances of granting and withholding assent to learn. In *Handbook of Curriculum and Instruction*, F. Michael Connelly, Ming Fang He, and JoAnn Phillion, eds. Thousand Oaks, CA: Sage, 198–218.

Esposito, Jennifer, and Ayanna N. Swain. 2009. Pathways to social justice: Urban teachers' use of culturally relevant pedagogy as a conduit for teaching social justice. *Perspectives on Urban Education* 6 (1): 38–48.

Fine, Michelle, Maria E. Torre, April Burns, and Yasser Payne. 2007. Youth research/participatory methods for reform. In *International handbook of student experience in elementary and secondary school*, Dennis Thiessen and Alison Cook-Sather, eds. Dordrecht, The Netherlands: Springer Publishers.

Fine, Michelle, and Lois Weis. 1998. *The unknown city: Lives of poor and working-class young adults*. Boston: Beacon Press.

Fobes, Catherine, and Peter Kaufman. 2008. Critical pedagogy in the sociology classroom: Challenges and concerns. *Teaching Sociology* 36: 26–33.

Gay, Geneva. 2010. *Culturally responsive teaching: Theory, research, and practice*. 2nd ed. New York: Teachers College Press.

Gold, Steven J. 2004. Using photography in studies of immigrant communities. *American Behavioral Scientist* 47 (12): 1551–72.

Gonzales, Norma E., Luis Moll, and Cathy Amanti, eds. 2005. *Funds of knowledge*. Mahwah, NJ: Lawrence Erlbaum.

Graziano, Kevin. 2011. Working with English language learners: Preserve teachers and photovoice. *International Journal of Multicultural Education* 13 (1): 1–19.

Greene, Jay, and Marcus A. Winters. 2006. *Leaving boys behind: Public high school graduation rates*. Civic Report #48. New York: Manhattan Institute for Policy Research.

Greene, Stuart, and Dawn Abt-Perkins. 2003. *Making race visible: Literacy research for cultural understanding*. New York: Teachers College Press.

Haddix, Marcelle, and Yolanda Sealey-Ruiz. 2012. Cultivating digital and popular literacies as empowering and emancipatory acts upon urban youth. *Journal of Adolescent and Adult Literacy* 56 (3): 192–98.

Hanley, Mary Stone, and George Noblit. 2009. *Cultural responsiveness, racial identity, and academic success: A review of literature*. Retrieved August 14, 2015, from http://www.heinz.org/UserFiles/Library/Culture-Report_FINAL.pdf.

Harper, Douglas. 2005. What's new visually? In *The Sage handbook of qualitative research*. 3rd ed. Norman K. Denzin and Yvonne S. Lincoln, eds. Thousand Oaks: Sage Publications, 747–62.

Herrington, Anne, Kevin Hodgson, and Charles Moran (Eds.). 2009. *Teaching the new writing: Technology, change, and assessment in the 21st century classroom*. New York: Teachers College Press.

Hetland, Lois, Ellen Winner, Shirley Veenema, and Kimberly Sheridan. 2007. *Studio thinking: The real benefits of visual arts education*. New York: Teachers College Press.

Hibbing, Anne N., and Joan L. Rankin-Erickson. 2003. A picture is worth a thousand words: Using visual images to improve comprehension for middle school struggling readers. *The Reading Teacher* 56 (8): 758–70.

Hicks, Troy. 2013. *Crafting digital writing: Composing texts across media and genres*. Portsmouth, NH: Heinemann.

Journell, Wayne, and Erin L. Castro. 2011. Culturally relevant political education: Using immigration as a catalyst for civic understanding. *Multicultural Education* 18 (4): 10–17.

Jurkowski, Janine M. 2008. Photovoice as a participatory action research tool for engaging people with intellectual disabilities in research and program development. *Intellectual and Developmental Disabilities* 46 (1): 1–11.

Kemmis, Stephen, and Robin McTaggart. 2000. Participatory action research. In *Handbook of qualitative research*. 2nd ed. Norman K. Denzin and Yvonna S. Lincoln, eds. Thousand Oaks, CA: Sage, 567–605.

Kress, Gunther, and Theo Van Leeuwen. 2006. *Reading images: The grammar of visual design*. New York: Routledge.

Kroeger, Stephen, Cathy Burton, Andrea Comarata, Cari Cobs, Christine Hamm, Randy Hopkins, and Beth Kouche. 2004. Student voice and critical reflection: Helping students at risk. *Teaching Exceptional Children* 36 (3): 50–57.

Ladson-Billings, Gloria. 2007. From the achievement gap to the education debt: Understanding achievement in U.S. schools. *Educational Researcher* 35 (7): 3–12.

———. 2009. *The dreamkeepers: Successful teachers of African American children*. San Francisco, CA: Jossey-Bass.

Lan, William, and Richard Lanthier. 2003. Changes in students' academic performance and perceptions of school and self before dropping out of schools. *Journal of Education for Students Placed at Risk* 8 (3): 309–32.

Lankshear, Colin, and Michelle Knobel. 2006. *New literacies: Everyday practices and social learning*. 2nd ed. Maidenhead, UK: Open University Press.

Lareau, Annette. 2003. *Unequal childhoods: Class, race and family life*. Berkeley: University of California Press.

Leu, Donald, Jr., Charles K. Kinzer, Julie Coiro, and Dana W. Cammack. 2004. Toward a theory of new literacies emerging from the Internet and other information and communication technologies. In *Theoretical models and processes of reading*. 5th ed. Newark, DE: International Reading Association, 1570–1613.

Lucas, Tamara, and Jaime Grinberg. 2008. Responding to the linguistic reality of mainstream classrooms: Preparing all teachers to teach English language learners. In *Handbook on teacher education: Enduring questions in changing contexts*. 3rd ed. Sharon Feiman-Nemser, D. John McIntyre, and Marilyn Cochran-Smith, eds. New York: Routledge, 606–36.

Marquez-Zenkov, Kristien. 2007. Through city students' eyes: Urban students' beliefs about school's purposes, supports, and impediments. *Visual Studies* 22 (2): 138–54.

Marquez-Zenkov, Kristien, and Jim Harmon. 2007. Seeing English in the city: Using photography to understand students' literacy relationships. *English Journal* 96 (6): 24–30.

Marquez-Zenkov, Kristien, Jim Harmon, Piet van Lier, and Marina Marquez-Zenkov. 2007. "If they'll listen to us about life, we'll listen to them about school": Seeing city students' ideas about "quality" teachers. *Educational Action Research* 15 (3): 403–15.

May, Stephen, and Christine Sleeter. 2010. *Critical multiculturalism: Theory and praxis.* New York: Routledge.

McClung, Merle S. 2002. *Public school purpose: The civic standard.* Bloomington, IN: Phi Delta Kappa Educational Foundation.

McIntyre, Alice. 2008. *Participatory action research.* Thousand Oaks, CA: Sage Publications.

Mediratta, Kavitha, Seema Shah, and Sara McAlister. 2009. *Community organizing for stronger schools: Strategies and successes.* Cambridge: Harvard Education Press.

Mitchell, Claudia, Relebohile Molestane, Jean Stuart, Thabsile Buthelezi, and Naydene de Lange. 2005. *Taking pictures/taking action! Visual methodologies in working with young people.* Retrieved August 14, 2015, from http://www.yahanet .org/sites/default/files/CHILDREN_FIRST_ARTICLE.pdf.

Mitra, Dana, and Steven J. Gross. 2009. Increasing student voice in high school reform: Building partnerships, improving outcomes. *Educational Management, Administration, and Leadership* 37 (4): 452–73.

Moje, Elizabeth, Melanie Overby, Nicole Tysvaer, and Karen Morris. 2008. The complex world of adolescent literacy: Myths, motivations, and mysteries. *Harvard Educational Review* 78 (1): 107–54.

Morrell, Ernest. 2007. *Critical literacy and urban youth: Pedagogies of access, dissent, and liberation.* New York: Routledge.

Noguera, Pedro A. 2008. The schools we need. In *The trouble with Black boys: . . . And other reflections on race, equity, and the future of public education.* San Francisco, CA: Jossey-Bass, 161–250.

Orfield, Gary, ed. 2004. *Dropouts in America: Confronting the graduation rate crisis.* Cambridge, MA: Harvard Education Press.

Orfield, Gary, Daniel Losen, Johanna Wald, and Christopher Swanson. 2004. *Losing our future: How minority youth are being left behind by the graduation rate crisis.* Cambridge, MA: Civil Rights Project at Harvard University.

Piper, Heather, and Jo Frankham. 2007. Seeing voices and hearing pictures: Image as discourse and the framing of image-based research. Special Issue: Beyond "Voice": New roles, relations and contexts in researching with young people, *Discourse: Studies in the Cultural Politics of Education* 28 (3): 373–87.

Raggl, Andrea, and Michael Schratz. 2004. Using visuals to release pupils' voices: Emotional pathways to enhancing thinking and reflecting on learning. In *Seeing is believing? Approaches to visual research*, volume 7. Christopher Pole, ed. New York: Elsevier, 147–62.

Rubin, Beth. 2007. "There's still not justice": Youth civic identity development amid distinct school and community contexts. *Teachers College Record* 109 (2): 449–81.

Rudduck, Jean. 2007. Student voice, student engagement and school reform. In *International handbook of student experience in elementary and secondary school,* Dennis Thiessen and Alison Cook-Sather, eds. Dordrecht: The Netherlands: Springer, 587–610.

Samuelson, Beth L. 2004. "I used to go to school. Now I learn": Unschoolers critiquing the discourse of school. In *What they don't learn in school: Literacy in the lives of urban youth,* Jabari Mahiri, ed. New York: Peter Lang, 103–22.

Schmakel, Patricia O. 2008. Early adolescents' perspectives on motivation and achievement in academics. *Urban Education* 43 (6): 723–49.

Seidl, Barbara. 2007. Working with communities to explore and personalize culturally responsive pedagogies: "Push, double images, and raced talk." *Journal of Teacher Education* 58 (2): 168–84.

Shah, Seema, and Kavitha Mediratta. 2008. Negotiating reform: Young people's leadership in the educational arena. *New Directions in Youth Development* 117 (8): 43–59.

Sleeter, Christine. 2008. Preparing white teachers for diverse students. In *Handbook on teacher education: Enduring questions in changing contexts.* 3rd ed. Marilyn Cochran-Smith, Sharon Feiman-Nemser, and D. John McIntyre, eds. New York: Routledge, 559–82.

Smith, John, and Lyn Fasoli. 2007. Climbing over the rocks in the road to student engagement and learning in a challenging high school in Australia. *Educational Research* 49 (3): 273–95.

Smyth, John. 2007. Toward the pedagogically engaged school: Listening to student voice as a positive response to disengagement and "dropping out"? In *International handbook of student experience in elementary and secondary school*, Dennis Thiessen and Alison Cook-Sather, eds. Dordrecht: The Netherlands: Springer, 635–58.

Streng, Matt, Scott D. Rhodes, Guadalupe X. Ayala, Eugenia Eng, Ramiro Arceo, and Selena Phipps. 2004. *Realidad Latina*: Latino adolescents, their school, and a university use photovoice to examine and address the influence of immigration. *Journal of Interprofessional Care* 18 (4): 403–15.

Stricklan, Martha J., Jane B. Keat, and Barbara A. Marinak. 2010. Connecting worlds: Using photo narrations to connect immigrant children, preschool teachers, and immigrant families. *The School Community Journal* 20 (1): 81–102.

Thiessen, Dennis. 2007. Researching student experience in elementary and secondary school: An evolving field of study. In *International handbook of student experience in elementary and secondary school*, Dennis Thiessen and Alison Cook-Sather, eds. Dordrecht: Springer, 1–78.

Torre, María E. 2005. The alchemy of integrated spaces: Youth participation in research collectives of difference. In *Beyond silenced voices*, Lois Weis and Michelle Fine, eds. Albany, NY: State University of New York Press, 251–66.

Van Horn, Leigh. 2008. *Reading photographs to write with meaning and purpose, grades 4–12.* Newark, DE: International Reading Association.

Villegas, Anna Maria, and Tamara Lucas. 2007. The culturally responsive teacher. *Educational Leadership* 64 (6): 28–33.

Wang, Caroline C. 2006. Youth participation in photovoice as a strategy for community change. *The Journal of Community Practice* 14 (1–2): 147–61.

Williams, Bronwyn T. 2008. "Tomorrow will not be like today": Literacy and identity in a world of multiliteracies. *Journal of Adolescent and Adult Literacy* 51 (8): 682–86.

Wilson, Nance, Stefan Dasho, Anna C. Martin, Nina Wallerstein, Caroline C. Wang, and Meredith Minkler. 2007. Engaging young adolescents in social action through photovoice: The youth empowerment strategies (YES!) project. *Journal of Early Adolescence* 27 (2): 241–61.

Yonezawa, Susan, and Makeba Jones. 2009. Student voices: Generating reform from the inside out. *Theory into Practice* 48: 205–12.

Zeller-Berkman, Sarah. 2007. Peering in: A look into reflective practices in youth participatory action research. *Children, Youth and Environments* 17 (2): 315–28.

Zenkov, Kristien. 2009. The teachers and schools they deserve: Seeing the pedagogies, practices, and programs urban students want. *Theory into Practice* 48: 168–75.

Zenkov, Kristien, Athene Bell, Marriam Ewaida, and Megan Lynch. 2012. Seeing how to "ask first": Photo elicitation and motivating English language learners to write. *Middle School Journal* 44 (2): 6–12.

Zenkov, Kristien, Anthony Pellegrino, Marriam Ewaida, Megan Lynch, Athene Bell, Corey Sell, and James Harmon. 2013. Picturing culturally relevant literacy practices: Using photography to see how literacy curricula and pedagogies matter to urban youth. *International Journal of Multicultural Education* 15 (2).

Zenkov, Kristien, and Jim Harmon. 2009. Picturing a writing process: Photovoice and teaching writing to urban youth. *Journal of Adolescent and Adult Literacy* 52 (7): 575–84.

Zumbrunn, Sharon, and Keegan Krause. 2012. Conversations with leaders: Principles of effective writing instruction. *The Reading Teacher* 65 (5): 346–53.

About the Authors

Kristien Zenkov, PhD, is a professor of education at George Mason University in Fairfax, Virginia. He is the author of more than one hundred articles and book chapters and six books on literacy, social justice, and teacher education. He codirects the Through Students' Eyes project—often partnering with teachers and students at TC Williams High School in Alexandria, Virginia—which calls on youth to document with photographs and writings what they believe about school, justice, and literacy.

Jim Harmon taught high school English, computers, and video production in the Cleveland, Ohio, area for eighteen years and is cofounder of Through Students' Eyes. He received his BFA in Photojournalism from the Rochester Institute of Technology and his MEd in Computer Uses in Education at Cleveland State University, where he was named a Distinguished Alumnus, 2008. Harmon was an adjunct teacher educator in educational technology at Baldwin Wallace University and Cleveland State University.

Acknowledgments

From Kristien: To Audra, for being the rock and friend and partner and love that I have longed to find, who enables this good work and this good life to an extent I have never before known. To my mom and dad, for being the first and best teachers in my life, for helping me to appreciate learning—not just school—in ways that I still count daily as a gift.

From Jim: To my wife, Karen, who never flinched at years dedicated to TSE, I am the luckiest guy on the planet. I love you! To my children, Tony and Cara, I hope this book serves as a reminder that hard work and passion in a life's work can make a difference, no matter how small. To my mom, thank you for always believing in me, in spite of my barely graduating from high school. To my coauthor, Kristien, this project and book would not happen without your laserlike focus on social justice, youth, and school. I am humbled by your work ethic, and delighted to call you my friend. And, finally, to all of the Cleveland youth who I have served in the past two decades: I have learned more from you than I have taught you, and you helped me realize a fundamental truth my mother first taught me: life may not take you where you want to be, but it takes you where you need to be.

From us both: To series editor Kay Adams, who pushed, prodded, cut, clarified, questioned, and deleted a lot: we thank you. And to those dear teacher

colleagues, especially Piet, Hannah, and Marriam, and all the activists/artists who have engaged with us and the Through Students' Eyes project youth as we have explored these adolescents' perspectives on school. To all of the students who we have had the amazing good fortune to know and work with as a part of the Through Students' Eyes project over the past dozen years—first in Cleveland and Euclid, Ohio, and since in northern Virginia, Sierra Leone, Haiti, Iraq, and India. We believe more with each interaction with you that you are the best informants for what schools and our teaching should look like, and that the only real future of education is one that makes listening to you an integral part of this thing we call "school."